BERNICE AND HER MULTIPLE PERSONALITIES

The human brain is a wonderful programable computer.
Reprograming the brain using hypnotherapy.

Zora O Young M.D.

authorHOUSE®

AuthorHouse™
1663 Liberty Drive
Bloomington, IN 47403
www.authorhouse.com
Phone: 1-800-839-8640

Published by AuthorHouse 1/23/2012

ISBN: 978-1-4678-5803-8 (sc)
ISBN: 978-1-4678-5802-1 (hc)
ISBN: 978-1-4678-5798-7 (e)

Library of Congress Control Number: 2011919817

CONTENTS

PREFACE

The reader may prefer to read the account of Bernice and her multiple personalities first, before reading these preliminary explanatory remarks which may then be read afterward.

INTRODUCTION

I am honored to be able to write this introduction for Zora Young, M.D. Dr. Young and I have been friends and colleagues for over 30 yrs. During the last few years we shared the same office.

In the late 1970's, I was fortunate enough to study with Milton Erickson, M.D. in Phoenix, Arizona. Not only did Dr. Erickson and Dr. Young have an extraordinary genius in their use of hypnosis, they both lived in the southwest and wore Native American turquoise.

In this book, Dr. Young uses hypnosis to treat a complex case of multiple personalities of a young woman. Actual cases of multiple personalities are rare and difficult to treat. In this case Dr. Young uses hypnosis to treat a patient with nine different personalities. Much of the communicating between Dr. Young and the patient consisted of letters that they sent to each other between their actual sessions. Dr. Young shows how hypnotic approaches were used to deal with conflicts the alters had at different periods of their development.

The reader will be shown how Dr. Young untangles a complicated multiple personality disorder with the use of hypnosis and supportive psychotherapy. It is sure to be an educational and fascinating read.

Philip Rich, M.D.

THE MENTAL COMPUTER

The mind is a naturally formed computer that is programmed to perform some functions automatically as regulation of vital functions. Other functions are learned by experience and education. A native language is learned which is used to communicate to others who share the language. The language is also used to formulate thoughts. Thoughts form beliefs. Beliefs influence our emotions and our behaviors. Examples of this are Galileo's belief that the earth was round and not flat which lead to the discovery of America and in the case of Bernice and her multiple personalities. The discovery that one of the sources of her miserable depression and low self esteem was a personality who believed she had killed three children. This personality was contacted in a state of trance by asking to speak to "where you feel you are not Loveable". A change in belief, lead to a dramatic change in Ruth, the personality. This illustrates how the mind can be reprogrammed. However, there may be resistance as demonstrated by a case reported in which "The Dictator" personality said " don't tell me what to do" very defiantly,

ON THE USE OF HYPNOTHERAPY

There are some conditions in which the mental computer malfunctions because of some abnormality in the functioning of the brain, in which case medication may be beneficial. Malfunction may be caused by structural abnormality. Hypnotherapy is not indicated in these conditions. Hypnotherapy is useful for psychogenic conditions when there needs to be a reprogramming of the mental computer. Hypnosis has been misunderstood and also abused as in staged demonstrations.

In his early work Sigmund Freud made use of hypnosis in the treatment of hysteria. It is reported that he ran into difficulty because he reported that some females with hysterical conditions reported they had been abused, particularlu in a sexual manner. His conclusions were contested and he adjusted his approach by accepting that the subjects were having wishful fantasies. More recent information indicates sexual abuse occurs much more frequently than previously believed and is frequently the trauma precipitating psychogenic mental illness. I reported two cases in the vignettes of this book. I have treated many more and hypnotherapy has been useful in these victims of abuse.

I hope to clarify misunderstandings of hypnotherapy. One is that suggestions have been the source of the reported findings rather than reality. I have honestly reported what I did and the changes resulting.. You may draw your own conclusions. In one letter I have included in this book the "Evaluator" discusses this issue and her assessment of the therapy and how we might try to test the reality of the results.

Information about physical computers may help explain how the mind functions. With the physical computer, information can be placed or recorded in the multiple programs ,which are called " files "on the computer, and this information can be accessed by contacting the program containing the information that is desired. Information is stored in different places in the mind, just as in the files of the mechanical computer. For example, certain things seem to be more likely to be on the left side of the brain than on the right side of the brain and vice versa. Also, information can be in what is called the "unconscious" part of the mind and is not immediately accessible to what is called the "conscious" part of the mind.

Hypnosis is shifting to the "unconscious" part of the mental computer where one can get information about programming and can suggest changes.

It is true that inappropriate suggestions can be made. The skill and trustworthiness of the operator may be compared to a surgeon performing an operation. The outcome should be the test of the effectiveness of the operation. In this book, I report the details of the effectiveness of using hypnotherapy. I compare this to what one does with the physical computer where information is stored and programs which can be accessed by properly choosing the program containing the information. The information can then be corrected, reprogrammed, if needed. The mind works much the same way, so fairly frequently, one can ask for information indicating what information is desired and request that the mind respond where this is known. The mind is able to hear and to respond to this kind of verbal request, but it may be necessary for the conscious mind to be turned off so that the part of the mind called the unconscious may be able to respond. When a part of the mind does respond language may be used to tell what is known there. This information may be accompanied by emotional responses that are appropriate to the content of the information disclosed. This may be difficult to believe and those who doubt this may say it was done by suggestion only. It is hoped, though, that the information provided in this book collected from the minds of the people with whom I used hypnosis makes sense out of the thoughts and feelings described and the origin of these in experiences. For example, a child-like part of the mind within Bernas believes that the dolls she killed were actual children and that they were alive and outside of her mind, and therefore that she had actually killed them. It was possible to restore these sources of consciousness to awareness and for the child to experience them, and able to talk to them.

Another example is that the part of her mind that hid under the porch or under the house complained that Dr. Young had not come to rescue her and after she was back to consciousness, another part of the mind with the name of Anne complained, "why did you bring this idiot back to bother us." As to the whether the hypnosis was beneficial, we have the outcome that Bernice was able to become comfortable and to function well enough to complete her education and to become a social worker who understood what it as like to be an orphaned child who needed a home and who worked to find appropriate homes for orphaned children. This fulfilled her frequently expressed wish to do something useful.

It is my belief that by hypnotherapy has been under-utilized and when it is properly utilized it can lead to effectiveness that seems miraculous and is very gratifying to the recipient and the hypnotist..

The human mind is a magnificent naturally formed computer which is programmed by inherited programming. Examples are walking and verbalizing (talking). We are taught a native language which is used to structure our thinking and communication. The wiring (neuronal) may be defective or the chemical support may be defective and medication may be effective. When the illness is a program problem, medication may affect the symptoms but not the cause. In the case of Bernice, the antidepressant prescribed was not effective and was potentially lethal and she took an overdose. She was so miserable and disappointed that a part of her took an overdose after she went to sleep. The report of her case as an example of the use of hypnosis is uncovering the programs in her mind and correcting them to restore health. Language is used to communicate with the sources of the multiple problems that need to be resolved. The use of words to program the mind has been called neuro-linguistic programming.

This will be explained by Richard Bandler and John Grinder in their books listed at the end of this book in the recommended reading section

Hypnosis is the mechanism of accessing the programs in the mind which is equivalent to clicking on a program or a file with the mouse in a computer. You can ask the "conscious" part of the mind to turn off and then ask a designated "unconscious" source of the information to turn on (become "conscious"). There is a difference from the mechanical computer because the mind is not mechanical and has a will and a choice. This is demonstrated by the "Dictator" in the case of Donna Lee and the "Dictator", the "Dictator" defiantly said "Don't tell me what to do!" Some people believe that multiple personalities are created by suggestions. Bernice believed that I suggested hers. I encourage you to consider whether I have "brainwashed" anyone inappropriately in what I have reported. I have made suggested interventions constructively with beneficial results. Bernice was very worried that I would produce conditions by 'suggestions "and that my diagnosis was in error about her having other entities which I called "personalities" and she believed I meant she had schizophrenia and she was "crazy" and that I would commit to a state hospital if she admitted she heard 'voices" which she believed would mean she had schizophrenia.

The phenomena of hypnosis have been abused to produce awesome effects by stage hypnotists which demonstrates the potential potency of hypnosis but frightens spectators. A great deal of trust is required of the subject toward the hypnotist comparable to that trust one makes when submitting to a surgeon operating on the heart or the brain.

Richard Bandler and John Grinder are pioneers in neuro-linguistic programming which is relevant to the interventions I report in this book. My findings as reported in the account of Bernice and her personalities were made in the 1960 to 1965 period long before I read Bandler and Grinder publications and was independent of their findings. They have written many very excellent books on the subject which you will find listed in Amazon.com and are recommend reading at the end of this book.

ON THE MULTIPLICITY OF THE"PARTS" OF THE HUMAN BRAIN.

The brain has areas that function to produce effects or functions. For example, vision and hearing. There are also areas that function in more subtle way. The "parts" may be sufficiently organized to justify being called "personalities." Examples in Bernice are the one I called the Evaluator who watched my moves and assessed the effects. Another, who called herself Anne, was the department of defense and intervened in an accident preventing a serious consequence. She also complained "why did you turn this idiot lose on us" when I rescued the child hiding under the porch.

Carl G. Jung recognized the presence of entities in the structure of the psyche and suggested that a symbol called a mandala having a circle with a center hub with spokes radiating out to the rim may have expressed the ideal of a central Self coordinating the entities at the rim. This idea prompted me to suggest to the Captain personality in Bernice that she might perform an integrative function since she knew all of the others.

The diagnosis of Multiple Personality Disorder is grouped in the Dissociative Disorders. Dissociation means a loss of the usual consistency and relatedness between various groups of mental processes, resulting in apparent independent functioning of one of them.(reference, Modern Synopsis of Psychiatry third edition page 243). This information may be used in understanding the cases reported in this book.

Vignettes

Brief examples of cases in which hypnosis was used

"I'M GOING TO DIE"

Hilda came to see me at the age of thirty-eight. She complained that her heart was racing and she felt like she was going to die. Her family physician had referred her because he had checked out her heart condition and found no physical disease of the heart and he felt that this was a physical reaction to her emotional condition.

Upon questioning, Hilda revealed that she was the mother of several children and a housewife. Her condition of rapid heartbeat and fear of death had begun in the recent months and had become increasingly worse. She felt there might be some connection with her son having had a recent tonsillectomy in which she feared he was going to die. Her overall sense of impending doom seemed to include that someone else in her family might die but was specifically related to her own concern that she was about to die. She did not know any conscious reason for this.

After exploring the events in her life I was unable to discover any reason why this should have occurred at this time. I decided that perhaps I could obtain more information by the use of hypnosis with her and with the use of hypnotic technique she went into a trance rather easily. I inquired about this feeling of death. I got this reply in a somewhat more childlike voice than she normally had. "I'm going to die."

I then asked, "Why do you believe that?"

She replied, "Because my mother died when she was thirty-nine."

I was puzzled by this connection with her mother's death at thirty-nine and thought that perhaps it was a frequent occurrence that people identify with their parents and expect the same thing to happen to them that happened to their parents.

I inquired further about this expectation to die at her mother's age.

"Why do you expect to die at your mother's age?"

"Because I promised God that I would die."

"Tell me about it," I inquired.

"Mother was dying and I promised God that if he would let her live, I would die in her place when I became her age."

"What happened that nearly caused your mother to die when she was thirty-nine years of age?"

"We were sitting out in back on a bench by the back steps. I got up off the end of the bench and it tipped with my mother and she fell backward and hit her head on the steps and I couldn't wake her up. She was dying and I prayed to God that she would live and I promised I would die in her place when I became her age and she woke up and lived."

"And now you feel that you're going to have to die because you made this promise?"

"Yes, it is coming time. I am thirty-eight years old and I am going to die soon."

I thought this over for awhile and replied, "Hilda, I do not think that God would require that you keep your promise. I do not think that he intended to have your mother die and that it was not necessary for you to promise to die in her place in order for her to live.

I think that when she hit her head against the steps she was knocked unconscious but she would have revived consciousness in a little while even if you had not made the promise. So I do not think that God would have found it necessary for you to have promised to exchange your life for hers and that he will not keep you to your promise and will let you live."

Hilda replied, "You mean that maybe he will not make me die?"

"I don't think he will because you have children who need you and I think he would like you to live and take care of them and see them grown up and even longer than that. I expect God will let you live a full life."

"How can I be sure of this?"

"Well, I suggest that you pray to God that he forgive you for making this promise as a child and that he will not hold you to it and that he will let you live. Tell him that you want to live to take care of your children and to be with your husband."

Hilda was silent for awhile and apparently was having her own silent prayer to God. In a little while she seemed to relax and be more comfortable.

I asked, "Do you believe that God will not hold you to this promise?"

"Yes, I think he's going to let me live."

I then returned Hilda back to her usual consciousness and asked her how she felt. She said the feeling of fear was gone and her heart was beating normally.

I asked that she come back the following week to see how she was doing. I told her if she had any difficulty in the meantime to feel free to call me.

Hilda returned the following week. She had continued to feel better and had not had any attacks of the rapid heart rate which doctors call tachycardia. I inquired whether there was any other problem in her life that she would like some assistance in resolving. She said that she cleaned her house very meticulously which involved considerable use of time and more than she would intend to do if she had her wishes about this. This seemed to be a compulsive behavior that she had to do and could not be comfortable unless she had done it.

I inquired about the possible roots of this behavior and she told me that her mother had been a very meticulous housekeeper and had kept her house spotless and that she had not wanted to be so careful as her mother although she did not want to be a sloppy housekeeper.

I again decided to check this out under hypnosis, feeling that I might be able to get through to this more easily and to make a more helpful change there.

While she was in a trance I asked Hilda, "Why is it that you feel you must keep your house as your mother did?"

She replied, "My mother was Dutch and she was taught to keep her house almost spotless. We even had a front stoop that was white and kept clean all the time. She swept it several times a day. When I promised that I would live in my mother's place until her age I also promised to be like my mother and that is what I am still doing."

"Yes, I do. I promised."

"Then I think we need to talk to God about this too because I do not think that he requires that you keep your house exactly as your mother did. I think that if you ask him that God will accept that you be able to keep your house in your own reasonable manner, reasonably clean and orderly but it does not have to be just as your mother kept hers and that he will let you have your own freedom to decide how to keep your own house."

"Do you feel it is necessary then to be like your mother?"

Hilda then asked, "You mean that I can ask him to let me keep my house the way I like to keep it?"

"Yes, I do, so go ahead now and tell him you would like to do that and would like his permission."

Hilda went silent for awhile, with her head bowed and then sat up again and said, "I think that will be alright now. I think I can keep my house the way I like to keep it and not like my mother kept hers."

"Fine," I said. "If you have any problem about this please let me know and we will see what we can do about it but I am sure you need not keep your house the way your mother kept hers. I think a reasonable amount of cleanliness and orderliness about the house is sufficient. There are other things that are important to do such as doing things with your husband and your children and having some time to enjoy your own life."

I then woke her from the trance and explained again to her what had happened in the session prior to this one and during this session. I told her that I believe it would be alright for her to be assured that she could live her full life without being held to the promise of dying at age thirty-nine and that she could keep her house the way that she liked to do it. I also stated that she was free to make her own decisions and not those of her mother, that her mother was not the deciding source of determining her behavior.

I told her if she had any more difficulty with these problems or any others to contact me and she thanked me and left.

HE IS THE ENEMY

John came to me at the age of thirty-five with these complaints:

"I have been getting headaches at work lately and I can hardly go on working. For a long time now I have also had difficulty sleeping because when someone slams a car door or makes some other sharp noise, I awaken startled and feel like I'm back in the war again."

"I also have another problem. I can't seem to keep from picking things up when I'm in a store, like pencils, fountain pens and other little things which I don't need, and I don't really understand why I take them and I'd like to stop this before I get caught."

I asked, "What happened in your life at the time or just before the headaches began?"

He said, "I keep thinking it has something to do with their assigning this Jap to work with me on the assembly line at the base. I find myself thinking that they are the enemy, what is he doing here? I feel I want to jump over the assembly line and strike him."

I asked, "How do you feel inside at the time he is there?"

"I feel very angry. I hate him. Could this cause me to have my headaches?"

"Yes, strong feelings like that, held inside, could cause a headache. Of course, you realize the war is over and he is no longer the enemy. Have you tried to get your mind to readjust to that fact?"

"Yes, I have, but it doesn't do any good, I just keep on feeling like he is the enemy and he shouldn't be there and I should attack him and get rid of him."

I said, "I guess we'll have to see what we can do but with your unconscious on this. Do you mind if we use hypnosis and see if we can get at the source of the distress toward this man?"

"Whatever will help, Doc," he replied.

"With his consent I helped him enter into a trance and I asked him how he came to be so angry at the Japanese.

This was his story:

"When I was on Corregidor when we surrendered, the Japanese came and rounded us up and took us for a long march to a port. On that march we did not have enough food or water. My cousin was in that group and he was feeling sick and when he couldn't go any longer and fell out they shot him.

I could have killed them for that but that wasn't all that they did. They crowded us into the hold of a ship, so packed together that if somebody fell down to the bottom there wasn't enough air there and he couldn't breathe and he died. So in order to say alive we had to stay awake and stay standing up for a very long trip. During that time it seemed I couldn't stay awake but somehow I did keep standing up. When I reached the port I couldn't remember all the time that had passed but I was still alive.

They took us to an island where they made prisoner of war camps and they assigned us to certain small tents, about eight people to a tent. They required that we live on rations that did not contain enough vitamins and we began to get sick from lack of certain vitamins. I worked on the docks and there we had to wear some large rubber boots. Whenever I got the opportunity I would sneak some vegetables from the produce we were handling, into my boots and take them back to my buddies and that way many of us were saved from having diseases which resulted in not having sufficient vitamins."

I interrupted him here and asked what the response of his buddies had been to his bringing back the vegetables with the vitamins in them.

He replied, "They were very happy with me and appreciated it very much because it kept us from dying."

I then asked, "Could this have something to do with your presently stealing things when you go into stores?"

"Yes, I guess it does. I got to feeling quite proud of myself, of being able to put one over on the Japs, of being able to steal something and get it back to my buddies. There were times I was not successful and they caught me and they whipped me for it, but I kept right on doing it anyhow."

I thought about this for a little bit and then said, "Perhaps you could decide that this is no longer necessary for your buddies and the matter of saving your lives by it is no longer necessary. It now threatens to give you difficulty without good reason which you did have when your buddies needed the vitamins. I wonder if you would give up doing this in order to save yourself from getting into trouble with the authorities, especially since it's not necessary any more. I realize this is a skill you learned and was very much rewarded by your fellow prisoners and it may be disappointing to you to give it up. I suggest that you might think about doing some magic tricks or something like that, that uses your slight of hand skill to conceal things, as magicians do, in order to compensate for this and that you might do this for your friends which would still give you pride in doing things without being seen and still get the approval of your friends for having done it. See if you can work this out some way so that you don't have to pick up things from the store and risk the chance of being arrested."

I asked him to continue with his story about the Japanese.

"They fed us out of tin cans with the lids still on them, like when you cut a lid off with a lid cutter and that was bent back and kind of used for a handle. One day a guard got mad at me and grabbed the can away from me and threw it in my face and the lid of the can cut my left eye and put my eye out. The left eye is now a glass eye. This made me very angry, it hurt and I did not get proper medical care and that's another reason why I hate these Japs.

"I asked, "There are times when you are sleeping and you hear something like a car door slam, what does that mean to you then?"

"It's like a shell going off, I mean it's like a mortar or a gun firing and I jump like I am being shot at."

"Inside do you feel like the war is still going on?"

"Yes."

"I think it's important in your mind that all of yourself realizes that the war is over. I would like for your mind that remembers your release at the end of the war to share with the rest of your mind that is apparently not fully aware of it, so while you tell me about it will you also, in your mind, listen and see and realize that the end of the war did come and it's over for now and we're at peace with the Japanese at this time."

I then asked him to remember the time when he was released from the prison camp and he said, "I remember when our troops finally came in and released us. We were half dead and we didn't think we were going to live, we were almost too sick to be happy about it, but it was a great day to get out of the prison camp. I remember their processing us and taking us to a hospital and then our being able to go back home again."

I asked, "Did the rest of your mind get the information about the end of the war, that it's over and we have now made peace with the Japanese."

He nodded his head and indicated that he had gotten the information.

I then said, "You will need to run this through your mind again and again until you realize the reality of it because you have to realize it and believe it in order to realize the war is over and that they no longer are our enemies, even though you may still feel angry at them, so I'd like for you to do that. Another thing that is going to be necessary is that you will need to go over the things you feel angry about and tell them to me and feel your anger with them and see if you can get your anger out so you won't be filled with anger that you had to hold in while you were their prisoner. That way I hope that will diminish the pressure of the angry feelings inside yourself and that you will become able to relax and feel comfortable, even though you have to work with a Japanese co-worker."

We followed this treatment plan and John reported that he was becoming more and more comfortable at work even though he was working with this Japanese co-worker and that he was able to relax more when noises sounded when he was asleep. He also reported that he was doing less of the taking of things in stores.

I felt that during this hypnotic sessions he sometimes was reacting to the sound of the typewriter of my secretary in the adjoining room, as if it were a machine gun. I felt this was an important circumstance, so that he could, right at that time, fully realize this was not a machine gun and identify it correctly as a typewriter and also, at the same time, realize that the war was over.

I said to him, "I notice you are responding to the typewriter as if it were a machine gun."

He nodded.

I said, "It is a typewriter and distinguish the difference between it and a machine gun. There must be some difference in the sound. Think about it and identify it as being the sound of a typewriter."

He nodded.

I said, "In addition to this I want you to recall immediately that when you hear a sound like this that the war is over so that it is not a weapon but some sound of industry or civilization such as a car door slamming or some other noise made in a peace time situation. Will you do that?"

He nodded.

In a fairly short time John reported that he was becoming comfortable at work, able to sleep without interruption, and he was no longer shoplifting.

With this we ended our sessions with my encouraging him to continue doing what he was able to do within himself and to continue his improvement and that if he had any difficulties or anything re-occur I wanted him to return to me and we would work on it.

THE CHICKEN NECK

Amy's complaint was "I was cutting up a chicken to cook it and when I had the neck in my hand, I got a panic feeling and threw it in the sink. Ever since then, I have been very anxious. I have no idea why this happened and why I can't get over it."

"I suspect that the chicken neck represented something that was frightening to your unconscious mind. Since you do not understand what the something is, the meaning must be known in your unconscious mind. I will ask your unconscious mind to think of the meaning and make it come to mind for you."

Amy agreed to the use of hypnosis, and after induction , I continued

.

" In your mind where you got scared of the chicken neck , think about what frightened you?.... What comes to your mind?"

"I see a child in the floor. It is like a picture in the floor."

"How old does she look to be?"

"She is about six or seven years old."

"I think this is a part of your mind that has withdrawn from consciousness. I suspect that something happened to cause her to disconnect or withdraw from consciousness. She is the source of the panic you felt and she knows what scared her. The chicken neck activated her. She is a part of your mind and is able to hear and to talk. I will see if I can communicate with her."

"Somewhere you're feeling scared. It's like you were scared stiff. You can hear me talking to you. I am a doctor who helps people who are scared and I want to help you. Please do not be afraid to listen to me. I am with you and I will protect you. You do not need to be afraid of me. I will not do anything to hurt you. I just listen and talk. I am outside here and there is no one else here. You are safe now. Whatever happened to you is not happening now. You may be afraid to look. I can look around for you and I see no one here but me and I did not do anything to frighten you, so it is safe for you to be here with me where I can help you. You may be too scared to look. Maybe you can just take a peek and see for yourself. I see that you are scared. You will be better when you see that what ever scared you is not here anymore. Be brave and dare to look. Good. You can see me now. Maybe it would help if you touched me. So you can tell I am really here. I see that frightens you. Did someone make you touch ? "

She nodded her head and began to cry.

"It's okay to cry. I will not make you do anything. I am with you to help you and you are safe with me. What happened?"

"A man came in the backyard and grabbed me and took me into the shed and hurt me. He said he would hurt my mother if I told anybody. You don't tell him I told you."

"I will not tell him. He has been gone a long time. He Is not coming back . You do not need to be afraid of him anymore. He scared you so bad that your mind stopped knowing what was happening outside to get away from him. It was like you went to sleep to get away from him. I woke you up. Another part of your mind stayed awake. Your body has been growing for so long that it has grown up now. You will be surprised as you learn all the changes that have occurred while you were asleep. I would tell your grown up self to teach you to understand what is happening now. The most important thing is that you are safe, and you are awake now. And you can learn how to live in your world now. I asked your grown up self to go to sleep so I could talk to you. I am going to wake her up now and she would take you home ."

"Amy, you have been in a trance while I talked with a part of yourself that blanked out when a man molested her when she was about six or seven years old. It is sort of like she went into a coma. It is a survival mode. That may happen in a crisis. She's going to be confused while she learns the changes that have happened in the here and now. You can be aware of her thoughts, and she can be aware of yours .In this way you can know what she is thinking. She can know what you are thinking. In this way you can teach her what she needs to know. I will be seeing you to follow up and help you."

Amy and her inner child successfully bonded and integrated. The anxiety subsided and there was increased enjoyment of life.

THE SMOTHERING BLACK

Betty came to me in the early 30s with a complaint that she felt depressed and anxious. I prescribed a serotonin reuptake inhibitor, which was of some benefit. She reported that she had a recurrent nightmare in which something black was smothering her. I suggested to her that we might be able to find out what that was about with the use of hypnosis and she agreed. She was able to go into a trance and I inquired for the source of this nightmare.

"Somewhere in your mind, you feel like you're being smothered by something black . You can hear me where you feel like you're being smothered by something black. I am a mind doctor. I help people who have trouble like you do, and I can help you. I only talk to people and do not do anything that hurts them. I will not do anything to hurt you. I will just talk with you. You are in my office room, and it is a safe place. You do not need to be afraid to talk. How old are you?"

"Seven."

"Where are you?"

"I am hiding in my cave."

"Who are you hiding from?"

"Father John."(Pseudonym).

"What has happened?"

"The sisters took me to him because I did something bad."

"What did he do to you?"

"He took off my panties and put his pants down and held me on his lap and pulled me up against him. I could not breathe . He hurt my wewe. I went in to my cave to get away from him."

"He is not here now. You do not need to hide any more. It is safe to come out now. Open your eyes and see that I am here. You do not need to be afraid of me. You do not need to be punished. You are not bad. You should not have been treated that way. You've got away from him by turning off what was happening outside. It is like you went to sleep, and you have been asleep for a long time. You can stay awake now. Another part of your mind woke up after this happened and knows what happened after that. I will explain to her that you have been asleep for a long time since it happened and you need her to help you understand what has happened during this time. She has grown up, and she will help you learn what has changed. Now I want her to wake up. Betty, wake up now. Take a deep breath and stretch. I have found out that you were molested by a priest and a part of your mind disconnected to escape from the trauma. The nightmare about being smothered in black is a flashback to that experience. I have awakened a part of your mind that went to sleep to escape and I have told her that the danger has passed and she is safe to be awake now. This part of your mind will be confused about all the changes in your life since you were seven years old. You will need to fill her in and orient her to your present situation. I will help you to do that. I believe you will be much happier and less anxious when she begins to be with you in the present."

The orientation was successful in that the depression and anxiety were diminished and the child was reoriented to the present.

The Screamer.

A woman in her late thirty years came with the complaint that she heard a child screaming in her mind. I asked her to let the screaming come out loud so we could find out what she was screaming about.

She said ". They will put me in a Napa (a state hospital).

I told her I could use hypnosis to find out what the screaming was about and assure the child that the danger was over.

I found that she had broken her wrist when she was seven years old she was anesthetized with ether which produced such severe stridor, a sound from obstruction of trachea or larynx, that the anesthetist stopped administration three times before she was out. She thought They were trying to kill her so apart of pretended not to be awake. She was so convinced that they would continue trying to kill her that I had a difficult time getting her see that they were no longer present. Finally she peeked out so slightly so " they would not know she was looking" and asked "Where is my father?"

I know it seems unbelievable that she had been in this suspended state for thirty years. She was unaware that her father had died. This an example of Post Traumatic Stress Disorder and how Bernice developed multiple personalities from the traumas in her childhood and adulthood as you will learn from her case study.

The "Dictator"

I was asked to see a woman in the hospital with severe back pain and no physical findings. She was 25 years old, married with two children. She was employed as a sales person in a music store. She had recurrent bouts of severe back pain with no evident cause.

I asked her if I could use hypnosis to find out if there was an unconscious cause of the pain. She agreed.

I induced a trance and asked:" Is there some place in your mind where you know what is happening to cause your back pain?"

In a younger voice she replied: "I'm just trying yo get out, that's all."

"Tell me about it"

"I'm trying to get out and I'm being held down."

I asked: "Is someone holding her down?"

A loud and gruff votce answered: "I am!"

"Why are you holding her down?"

"Because I've got the power."

"if you are doing just because you have the power. You are acting like a dictator.

You should use your power with yourself. I will explain how."

In an angry defiant voice: "Don't tell me what to do!"

I decided this was too complicated to try a quick resolution and diagnosed the problem as "psychogenic and recommended discharge.

I asked her to call my office and make an appointment to begin psychotherapy.

Therapy revealed that as a baby she had ear infections with severe ear aches. On three occasions her parents held her down so the doctor could lance her ear. On the last occasion she struggled so hard that her parents could not hold her still and she felt the power of defeating her parents and the doctor who "wanted to hurt" her for no reason she understood. She felt betrayed and angry.

I explained the situation now that she understood words. This altered her feeling of betrayal by her parents. She was able to accept my advice as a choice and to try working with herself. She was so successful that she became the owner of a thriving business selling musical instruments.

BERNICE AND HER MULTIPLE PERSONALTIES

Bernice was shocked when she awakened on the intensive care ward in the hospital. She called to the nurse: "What am I doing here?"

"Don't you know?"

"No I don't."

"You took an overdose of your antidepressant medication."

"I did not take an overdose of my medication."

"Well, your records say the bottle was empty. The emergency room had to pump your stomach and put in charcoal. They say if you had not called for help, you might have died.

Beatrice was puzzled. She did not remember calling for help or taking an overdose of her medication. She did remember taking the usual dose of medication and going to sleep. She decided to wait until her doctor came to ask more questions.

When her doctor came he smiled and said, "You are awake! How are you doing?"

"I am a little bit groggy and I have a headache. I do not remember taking all those pills. I took the right amount and went to sleep. The next thing I know, I woke up here"

"You damn near died. Something very serious happened. I want you to see a psychiatrist who will help you sort this out. I want you to see Dr. Young. He will help you find out what's going on."

Bernice procrastinated about calling me after she returned home. She said she was frightened that I might think she was crazy, but if she did not get help, she might kill herself. She had called and made appointments twice and canceled them and kept a third appointment. She had brown eyes and hair; and was neatly dressed in a white blouse and brown skirt and appeared to be anxious and depressed. I asked her the usual questions for information. She was twenty-nine years old and married with four daughters and two sons. She had graduated from high school and was taking some courses at community college. She did not remember her childhood before the age of seven at which time she was living with her sister and brother-in-law. She had been told that her mother died of cancer when she was five years old. Her father had remarried. She told me that she must have taken an overdose of medication but she did not remember taking it. She said she had taken the correct dose and gone to sleep. She awoke in the hospital the next morning. I asked about her symptoms.

"I have periods of being depressed and moody with a lump in my throat. Sometimes I cry without it making any sense. I don't like for the children to see me this way .It makes them moody too. I go to bed and then have the bigger children keep the little ones away until I feel better. All of a sudden I may feel better and get up. I get to where I can be a normal person and laugh and be happy and then these extremes come on .Sometimes I feel I'm not worth anything. Not even the oxygen I breathe. Life just doesn't seem worth living. And if I didn't have children,

I would have committed suicide in a long time ago. Yesterday and today I feel like living. Before, then I wanted to die. We have no real worries, no reason for a person to get blue and depressed. I get irritable and hard to live with. I don't want to even talk to my husband. As long as no one bothers me, I'd just wait until I get it out of my system. I feel unworthy of anyone's love and feel unloved. When depressed, I eat more than I

should, I don't enjoy it but it seems to help put off the worst. I guess we don't feel proud of ourselves when we indulge in food.

I have thought an awful lot about going insane. I guess I hadn't realized just how severe insanity is. I thought I was a manic depressive, until I asked a man who works in a mental hospital how they acted and realized I don't have the extremes.

I have bad dreams and often wake up shaking. I am afraid of the dark. Sometimes I would dream that I hear the door open, and hear footsteps, and it seems so real that when I woke up, I used to go check the door, but I don't check anymore. A recurrent dream is that I am choking and can't get any air. It's like I'm being dragged through the air, as if it is all going to be over in a few minutes and just when I'm going to gasp for the last breath, I wake up. There is no reason for a person to get blue and depressed. I get irritable and hard to live with. I don't want to even talk to my husband. As long as no one bothers me, I'd just wait until I get it out of my system.

I write stories, fiction sometimes based on facts. Sometimes I write essays. I did write one story based on a dream that I was carrying a tiny baby. It was raining, and I was surrounded by a bunch of dogs who were vicious. They were pulling at my coat, tugging at the baby's blanket. I woke up just when the dogs are about to take me apart."

"Do you go over difficult unhappy memories?"

"I have been doing that recently. Like when I was five. I can remember a number of things about mother when she was sick before her death. She died of cancer, but I can't remember a thing about the funeral. In those days at that little town, the bodies were kept in the home. All I can remember is a pine box, like the kind they put caskets in. I know I was at the funeral, because my sister has a snapshot of me there. People were morbid in those days and took pictures of things like that."

Bernice said these things without any emotion.

"What do you think when you're in these moods?"

"About how I can get out of them. I have thoughts of being unworthy and of committing suicide."

"Have you ever attempted suicide?"

Bernice hesitated in answering this question. She seemed to struggle with her answer.

"No. I have not. My doctor who referred me after I woke up in the hospital told me I had taken an overdose of my antidepressant pills. I had gone to sleep the night before, and they said I had called for an ambulance and said I had taken an overdose of my medication. I don't remember doing that. I would not try to kill myself because of the children. I guess I did it in my sleep. I am afraid you'll put me in the hospital if you know this, but I'm afraid I might do it again. Do you think I should be in the hospital?"

"It does worry me. I will find out more about what happened that night."

"How would you do that?"

"I can use hypnosis to find out what happened when you were sleeping. Somewhere in your mind you took the pills and somewhere in your mind you called an ambulance. I would like to know if the same part of your mind that took the pills also called for the ambulance or whether it was some other part of your mind that called the ambulance. Hypnosis is a natural ability of your mind to focus the sources of consciousness. Are you willing to do this?"

"Are you sure it's safe?"

"Yes, your mind has natural protection. I will begin by asking who called for help.

That way, I will contact the part of your mind that wants to live. Close your eyes and imagine that you're going down 10 steps to a beach. There are 10 steps going down to the beach. The top step is number 10. I will count down one step at a time for you and when you reach the bottom one you will sit down and look at the ocean. Going down now, ten nine eight seven, six, five, four, three two, one Now sit down on the step and look out at the ocean. Imagine you see seagulls circling over the water. Feel how peaceful and comfortable you are. Enjoy your trip to the beach without being distracted when I talk to another part your mind.(Pause) Somewhere in your mind, you called for help after the pills were taken. I want you to hear me there and you will be able to talk to me as you were able to call for help. You can awaken now and talk with me."

The eyes opened and a smiling, youthful face appeared. She waved her hand in a greeting .

"Hi. I'm Nancy, I finally got her here. She canceled twice. I called for the ambulance. I wanted to save the body. If she didn't want it, I did. I want to live. I hope you can help her want to live too. The one I call the maid took the pills to kill herself. She wants to die. I came back to help her."

"What do you mean you came back, were you here before?"

"Yes, I came after her mother died. My uncle was the doctor who tried to save her mother. He brought me to spend the summer with Bernas. She was very lonely. We played all summer and had a happy time. At the end of the summer, I went home. But I was still with her too but I did not have my own body. I was in her body with her. We still talked and played together. She wanted me to have everything she had. When her Papa bought her a parasol, she would not open it until Papa bought one for me too. Hers was blue. Mine was red. She set a place at the table for me. I really didn't care about having a parasol or place at the table, but she insisted."

"Who is Bernas?

"That is what her name was before she changed it to Bernice."

"When did you go away?"

When her stepmother came to live with us, she told her Papa that she was crazy for hearing voices and she just wanted to get two of everything and so she pretended I was real. She made him make her stop talking to me and I went away."

"Where did you go"

"I don't know. I guess I just laid away on the other side. When I found out she was so unhappy, I came back to help her. I don't know how to help her. I urged her to come to you. Do you think you can help her?

"I think I can. I want you to be her guardian angel and keep her safe. So I will have time to work with her. Will you keep her from killing herself?"

"Yes, I will."

"I will be talking with you again. Let me talk to Bernice now. Bernice, you can wake up here now. Wake up when I count to three for you."

Bernice woke up and asked, " What happened?"

"I talked with the part of yourself who called for help. Her name is Nancy. She came to spend the summer with you after your mother died. Nancy went home at the end of the summer, but your mind must have re-created her because she has existed in your mind since that time. We can reproduce a person in our mind, We call it incorporation. Nancy did not take the pills. She called the ambulance. A third person Nancy called 'the maid' took the pills and Nancy called for help."

"I'm not crazy."

"Who said you were?"

"You did. You're saying I have a split personality. That means schizophrenic. Having schizophrenia means being crazy. I'm not crazy."

"You are right. You do not have schizophrenia. You have multiple personalities. You have at least three personalities including your own. This condition is not a psychosis or craziness, something must've happened in your childhood which resulted in your mind dividing into several parts. We will find out what happened and make corrections."

"I do not accept your hypothesis. I do not have three personalities. Can you give me some medication and not get into this issue about personalities?"

"Medication works if the condition is a biochemical one. This condition is not a biochemical one. Some things have happened in your life that ended up with your mind in pieces and we can get them back together again. I can do this. I have done this with others and can do it for you. In the meantime, Nancy will guard against the maid killing herself and you and Nancy. Ask my secretary for a return appointment and I will see you again next week."

When she returned the next week, I asked her, "How has your week been?"

"I still feel depressed. I read about hypnosis and it said that suggestions can be made that a hypnotized person takes to be reality. How am I to know whether you are making such suggestions?"

" I am careful not to make suggestions. I choose information such as the fact that you did not call for help, but there was a call for help. I then asked for more information to understand what was happening in your mind. If there is an error in thinking, I explain to your mind the error that I detect. Your mind may or may not choose to change the belief. I accept your reservation about whether to trust me. I promise not to put any suggestions into your mind. I realize this is difficult to trust someone tinkering with your mind while you are unconscious but it is really more safe than having a surgeon operate on your body when you are under anesthesia because your mind has a warning system that is on guard that will wake you up if there is a danger. That is why you woke up in the dream about those vicious dogs just before you were bitten and woke just before your 'last breath' when you dreamed you were choking to death. You may need to have time to get to know me better before we proceed . What do you want to do?"

"I guess I'll just have to trust you. Go ahead."

"All right, I want your unconscious to know you can awaken at any time I ask you to do anything which you do not want to do, Now close your eyes and relax and go into a trance while I count for you. You will return to the beach as you did before. I counted her down to the beach as I have before, and then I paused and said]:"Somewhere in your mind you are able to be aware of what is happening when you are asleep or in a trace. I want you to listen in and to feel free to object to any thing I suggest if you so choose. You are in the center of your consciousness and I want you to know what I am doing and you may bring to my attention issues to which you want me to attend to. Now I want to talk to Nancy.

" Nancy, I would like to speak to you."

Nancy did not awaken. The body showed evidence of tension and a struggle. After a few minutes I said. "Nancy, relax and let me find out what is happening. The struggle stopped and the eyes opened and she said:

"I want to talk. I was here first"

"Okay. Who are you?"

"I am Bernas. I took those pills because I feel so bad. They weren't doing any good anyway. I won't go on living this way. The only way out is to die."

"I know there's another way out. I can help you. I am sure this unhappy feeling has been happening for a long time, and you have gotten discouraged because nothing has changed all this time. With your help, I will find out what is wrong and we will correct it. First of all, I want to know if you would agree to wait and see what we can do to change something for the better. Will you agree to that?"

"Yes"

'How are you troubled?"

"I have a lot of troubles. Sometimes I dream I have a heavy tote sack on my back and I'm so tired I can't go on. I feel very guilty as if I have done something terribly wrong but I don't know what it is and I feel like I don't deserve to live. I don't know what I have done that was so wrong. I think no one wants to be my friend. She has taken over my life and the only time I get out is when there is housework to do. I do housework, that is all I get to do. I feel very lonely. I think no one wants to be my friend."

"Let us begin by talking about the bag of troubles. We will talk about the feeling that you don't deserve to live. Somewhere in your mind, you have reasons why you don't feel like you deserve to live. Why do you feel that you do not deserve to live, I want you to tell me why you don't feel like you deserve to live."

"My mother died because I wasn't good enough for her to live."

"Why do you believe that you were not good enough for her to live?"

"Because I prayed to God that I would be very good if my mother would live. She died because I could not be good enough. Even the doctor could not save her. He tried every medicine he could get. When she died, he smashed the bottles on a rock and said,' I'm very sorry, Bernas, I did all I could to save your mother' I think it was my fault because I wasn't good enough. I don't think I'm good enough for anyone to love me

"It was not your fault, Bernas. She did not die because you're not good enough. She died of cancer and it was no one's fault. Children often think that they have caused something to happen. You must change your thinking about this. It was not your fault. It was not because you were not worth living for. You were mistaken to think that if you were good enough your mother would live. Some things happen that are no one's fault. There are some things no one can do anything about. I believe even God could not do anything about saving your mother from the cancer. Her very good doctor could do nothing about it either. And as a child, you certainly could not do anything about it. You know you so much wanted your mother to live and did your very best to be good, and you were good. Now you must change your thinking so that you do not think that your mother's death means you weren't worth living for. You are a good girl, and you are lovable and worth living for and caring about. Please believe this. Believe you are loveable and a good girl.

Will you believe you are a good and loveable girl?"

"Yes.

Now can you think of any other reason why you think you weren't worth loving and living for?"

"My papa didn't want me. He made me go away."

"He should not have done that. Your stepmother made him do it. She was a mean stepmother. She convinced your father you would be better off with your sister. And she told him not to even let you take your dolls with you. She stopped you from being able to talk with your friend , Nancy . She was an old witch. She got control of your father. Your father should not have chosen her instead of you. He made a bad choice. You are worth loving and should've stayed in your home. You are a good girl. Your father should have kept you at home. It was the old witch's fault. You have the right to hate her. It does not mean that you are not worth loving. You are worth loving. You can believe you are loveable because I am telling you so and I am a very wise doctor, like a wizard, so believe me. Can you think of another reason why you think you're not worth caring about?"

"Herman, my brother-in-law, who said I was an ugly, snotty nosed kid, who was good for nothing and nobody would want me."

"Don't believe what he said. It was unfair and a very bad opinion and he should not have said that of you. You are not ugly and you are good for many things, much more than just housework for which you are very good. You also took care of your little niece for your sister. I think they did not tell you how helpful you were. They did not tell you enough how much you should have been appreciated. Children need to be told they are doing very well and that their help is appreciated and they should have done that for you. Your mind needed that kind of nourishment just like your body needs food to grow up feeling healthy. I am giving you some of that praise now and I want you to take it in, eat it up and I am telling your other selves right now to feed you love and appreciation so you can feel OK. I want you to believe you are okay.

I told the one that scolds you to quit saying bad things to you and that will help you feel good and you will make everyone feel more happy. I want all of yourself to hear this, I know it's frustrating to you that Bernas feels so unlovable. You can help her by telling her you will love her and you can help her feel loved and she will stop your feeling unhappy. She does the house work and does it very well and you should appreciate that this gives you time to do other things you want to do with the time she saves for you. Give her hugs and tell Bernas how much you appreciate her, Bernas, Nancy is your friend and she is with you now to help you. You can talk with her again and I will tell her to help you feel okay. I want to speak with Nancy now.

(Pause) Nancy, I want you to be able to know what Bernas and I have been talking about. I want you to be able to know what we said, and for you to talk to Bernas , like I have, to assure her that she is lovable and is a good girl. I want you to assure her that she is lovable and a good person. Is there anything you want to say?"

"Yes, I'll tell you about a dream I had. A child is hiding behind a big rock. I recognize the rock . Bernas and I used to play around it. I thought I should tell you the dream."

"I think your mind gives you dreams like this to tell us to pay attention to someone who needs help. One patient I helped dreamed there were children of hers who were at the bottom of a swimming pool and she was bringing them to me and I was resuscitating them. I was able to contact them and bring them back to life. We will see what we can do for this one."

"Let your mind shift to where you are hiding behind a big rock. Some where you are hiding behind a rock. Why are you hiding there?"

"I'm hiding from Papa."

"Why are you hiding from him?"

"He wants me to get in the car and go away. I won't go and I ran here to hide from him."

"He is gone now. You stopped knowing what was happening outside. You stopped feeling your body and you stopped seeing with your eyes. Much time has passed since then. I am Dr. Young, and you are in my office. You are safe here. I want you to open your eyes and look around. Open your eyes now. "

She opened her eyes and looked around in surprise.

"I am Dr. Young, and you are in my office. You have been asleep a long time. Many years have passed while you were sleeping. Your body has kept growing while you were sleeping, and it has grown up now. You're in a different place now. You can see you're not behind the rock now."

"I want to go home."

"The home you were in was a long time ago and is far away and you have a new home now. "

"I could walk."

"It is much too far to walk but you have a new home that is near here and you can go to it. Your grown-up self will take you there. Your grown-up self will take care of you. You are safe to go back to sleep now. Go back to sleep. "

(Pause) Bernice, wake up now as I count to three. One two three. Stretch now. (Pause) I've been talking to a child who has been hiding behind a big rock. And she wants to go back to her old home. I told her you will take her back to the new home. If she wakes up tell her, she is with you now that you will take care of her.

"Is this one of your suggestions?"

"No, she is very real. Call me if there are problems with her. I will see you next week. Goodbye."

Bernice called me three days later.

"I keep hearing this child's voice saying 'I want to go home'. This is driving me up a wall. Do something."

"I will ask Nancy to work with this child, help her accept this new home. Nancy, listen, talk to this child and help her. Tell her not to be afraid and that you will take her home when you can take her there and that she can live in this home until then. You can be like a foster mother to her. If this does not help, call me again."

I thought of the proverb to let sleeping dogs lie. I wondered if I should have awakened this child at this time. I thought the source of the dream was presenting her to me for assistance at this time but I could have waited. It is my intention to determine whether there is sufficient distress originating from a source to justify an intervention. I did not determine that in this instance, I think I should've waited until I had more time to talk to her.

Bernice asked me to see her husband because she believed he was a significant source of her problems. I did see him. He was an electrician, who was satisfied with his own mental health, and did not see any need for a change. I offered him an option of seeing a psychologist for marital counseling, and did not choose to accept that. He did not have the motivation to participate. Bernice brought up her concern about their problems on several occasions during her treatment and I repeatedly explained to her that since he did not have the motivation more could be gained by resolving her problems than spending the time working with him.

Nancy told me later that she told the child if she would go to sleep, she would wake her up when it was time to go back home.

The secretary left me a note: "Bernice came in. Says she has no knowledge of what has been going on or what she might have said or done. Since her husband told her last night that she had canceled her appointments, etc.. Up until then, she thought she had an appointment tomorrow at 2;oo as usual. She wanted to come by and apologized for anything she might said or done to either of us. Says we have really been most helpful and she does appreciate all. Feels she must be flunking her school work as she does not remember about it either". This is an example of periods of amnesia. An alter was doing the schoolwork efficiently.

Nancy wrote an account of her awakening.

The awakening

"I became aware of life again in 1951. It was the strangest darn feeling. You can imagine. The numbness of deep sleep gradually left me with only a slight dizziness remaining. I stood by a .white range in a small neat kitchen. In my hand was a spoon, and I was stirring some kind of yellow custard on the stove. There was a good smell of food and it was noisy with the sound of childish voices. L looked around for my little friends. I felt so large, so awkward. It was utterly strange. A little table was set for the talkers. Where were my friends? My Bernas Ruth? The little girl and boy at the table were putting together a puzzle of large heavy pieces .I left the stove and walked to them. "Hello" ,I said, looking down at them. I did not comprehend entirely that I was grown up, that I was no longer a child myself.

"Mama, see the duck?"The boy grabbed my hand and pointed to the shape of one of the pieces of the puzzle. His eyes were soft brown and his baby face was topped with brown curls. I wanted to touch his small hands, but the little girl claimed my attention:"Mama!" She pushed back her chair, her blond curls bouncing, and she ran across the room, "The pudding is burning." Her tiny hands turned the knob on the stove and the fire went away under the pan. The food was smoking. I now realized I had completely forgotten the pudding. She looked at me with a quizzical look. Her eyes were as blue as the boy's were brown. She looked like a fairy with a short blue pinafore over a white dress and a blue ribbon tied in her hair. But she was calling me momma ! She waited as I continued to orientate myself to the situation. She picked up a potholder and pulled the pudding off the stove and put the smoking pan in the sink. "Mama, why did you let the pudding burn?"I felt foolish that this little girl should be assuming the role of an adult but suddenly I felt awareness fading, as I drifted out of existence and heard a hysterical sob coming from within, a deep dry cry that I did not recognize. I knew I did not own this large stranger body like the last sharing of a body with Bernas Ruth. I now had been in an adult's body in a strange room, with little children and now this adult was claiming her body.

Most people are born as an infant. They grow and develop in a body of their own.

But some of us, it seems are in a body that belongs to someone else. It just happens. I was such a child coming to life gradually in the mind of a child, who was in need of a playmate in forested foothills in the Appalachian mountains. I fought and struggled for air. The children were staring with large eyes They were frightened and I wanted to reach out to them but the hands were not mine. The voice had broken into a sobbing and the strange person was running from the room and I felt no more.

Time is such a funny thing when you don't have it consistently. And I had never been used to continual awareness. So I could accept the short intervals of time that were mine from time to time. Life puzzled me for some time, for I was in a different world now from the one I had known as a child on the farm. But my intervals of time were so infrequent that it must've taken months for me to figure out where I was and what part of the country I lived in. I greatly disliked this party with whom I shared the body. She was certainly far from a cheerful person to be around. Usually, she was in tears or staring moodily out of the crack in the Venetian blinds. The children are always immaculate and while they were happy enough I knew that this person, who was their mother was often puzzling and frightening to them. As I continued to awaken from time to time it became easier for me. I would become aware of the situation at hand, much as a person stepping into the room. I could feel the emotions of the person who had the body and I could observe her as another person by her emotions rather than by sight of course. I very definitely did not like her emotions! At first I thought she was the stepmother that had caused Bernas Ruth to have to leave home, but the children were here, where was Bernas Ruth?

One day I became aware of this creature lying across a bed. She was sobbing with horrifying, dry sobs. Her hands were clenched into knots and her face was twisted and contorted as she tried to refrain from crying. She was so distressed, that I felt I should help her as I struggled for air of my own. She grabbed her head, and the thoughts that flashed through her mind. Made me laugh in spite of my concern for her. She had grabbed her head and sat up right in the bed. "Oh God." She said with genuine reverence, "God, please protect me from these demons. Oh, dear Jesus don't let them take me away." Suddenly I took things away from her as well as I could, and she was no more. I thought I had the body again and I liked it. I wanted to keep it. I liked the air and feeling. I went to the mirror and looked at the body. Well it certainly wasn't beautiful but perhaps it could be worse. I picked up the small calendar from the chest.

November 1951 Ye gads,I thought. I have been somewhere for at least 15 years! I looked at the room and felt more freedom from the other person . I was completely calm and began to look for the children. I went into another bedroom and found them sleeping in their two small beds. The girl had kicked aside her blanket so I covered her up again. I left them to look at the rest of the house. I found a most delightful change in so many things. A small bathroom with gleaming white fixtures, reminded me of the outdoor privy and round washing tub of past years. I picked up the brush and brushed the hair, my hair? Well for the moment it was. So I brushed it out and up and felt wonderful. I smelled of the soap and a bottle of perfume found in the medicine cabinet. I'm sure that a man also was here, for his shaving articles were there. Somehow this excited me and I felt great potential as a human being! I opened closed blinds in the living room, not bad at all. There were trees outdoors with a green lawn and paved street, not a bad improvement in living conditions. After I had thoroughly inspected the house, I felt restless. I wanted to know who this person was that I was sharing a body with. And I wanted to know where I was and what my possibilities were but then the strangest darned thing happened. I knew my stomach was too large and heavy. When I sat down to decide what next to do, I felt the strangest sensation. Something moved inside. I put my hand over my abdomen, and suddenly a knot appeared like a lump on her stomach. I somehow comprehended there was an unborn child inside. I thought this over and tried to decide how I felt about being pregnant. I had seen a pregnant woman once when Bernas Ruth and I lived together. She was large and awkward. Bernas Ruth had whispered about it to me, but I failed to see anything funny or shameful about it ,If a baby grew inside an adult that seemed a reasonable way to be born after all, I was always inside a body and it seemed it wasn't too different except the lucky baby had his own body growing that could someday be its own body. If I had a body growing, I had never known it. I was only a part of a body ,dammit! I wanted my own body, perhaps I would keep this one but I felt sleepy, and I still didn't know who the person was and that owned the body. I would ask the children when they woke up. But now I was drifting into oblivion. I had no particular desire to struggle for air. It was easier just to relax. I somehow, I knew, I would return again some other day so I went without a fight for the body. I guess I'm not really a fighter for I hate struggle and even today,I find it easier to drift with the tide than to battle the current. Relax and enjoy life is my greatest delight. I still think it is the only way to live. I love life. In this world, I believe I have it to keep now. I do feel frustrated by some that are a part of me. I must accept them and live with them ,however , and perhaps they will improve. They may be able to enjoy life also.

I had another glimpse of life in December. It was Christmas Eve and I could feel this person I shared the body with. She was very tense and tears were falling from her face as rain might from a cloud. She was standing rigidly and trying to do something with her hands. She was holding some metal object. Why was she so afraid? I tried to see what was going on and this must've given her some kind of pain for she muttered something about " my head." And threw down, what she held in her hand to grab her head. And his voice was swearing at her with a sound of contempt.

"Your head ! You do nothing but complain!"

This angered me. Why should anyone talk to this person as if she were an animal? I stepped into the body as she went out with a primitive sob. I blurted out.

"You have no right to talk like that!" I found myself facing a man I had not seen before. He jerked his head up and glared at me with cold blue eyes. He was disgusted and had no patience in his features.

"How can you tell me what I have no right to say!" Obviously, he was not accustomed to contradiction.

"I won't be talked to like an animal." I said and I meant it. No person should be spoken to with such a tone of voice"

.

"Oh, you won't. Then hold this right and shut up"

He thrust a piece of maroon metal at me and I ignored it.

"I'm not ready " I said and I wasn't. I didn't know what was going on and I needed time to orientate myself so I turned from him in the clumsy **swolen** body and walked to a chair where I sat as gracefully as I could and surveyed the room. A Christmas tree! And toys! I was intrigued and then couldn't resist going over and picking up a doll in a blue dress. She cried. How beautiful her dress was! A little box played music when it was turned. Packages with ribbons were under the tree. A large bicycle was assembled, and I could see the frustrated man was in the process of putting together another one. Then I knew what they had been doing when I awoke. Oh that would be fun ,I felt so, I dropped to my knees beside him and said "Here, let me help you." He glanced at me with contempt.

"Get out of my way." He growled.

"Well you're not very nice." I said. "I only want to help!"

He gave me an odd look and resumed to work. I looked him over, and I certainly did not know him. He was blonde and not as large as Popa had been. He was such a mere boy really. I could not help from laughing. It seemed so very funny when I thought how he had mistaken me for his wife!. He was aware that I watched him with amusement, and his anger seemed to dissipate and he was almost cordial by that time, Th piece of equipment was assembled. I might as well go along as if I belonged here, I decided. So I went to see about the children. They were sleeping in pink and blue pajamas. So I was pulling the covers over them when the man hissed at me to "get the hell out of there before you wake them up." He grabbed my wrist rudely and pulled me toward the door

"For Christ's sake, woman, if you expect to get any sleep tonight, we better get it now before they wake up."

Sleep? I had just woke up so I told him "no thank you", politely, of course. "I really don't feel like sleeping right now."

"What's gotten into you?"he demanded.

I laughed. This funny man. What he really meant was what's gotten into her. Everything was gay and lovely, and I felt bubbling with excitement. I wanted to watch the lights on the tree go on and off. And I wanted to go outside and see the stars again and the beauty of the night.

"I'll take a walk now I told the man. Could you help me find a coat?" He looked for a moment again as he would explode but I kept smiling at him and he ended with a half smile.

"Now come on, and let's go to bed. You're acting sort of funny." I felt the tug from inside. "This baby inside me is getting pretty big, isn't it?" I said, fishing for information. I was also trying to converse with the man and not anger him.

"Yes". He was a man of few words. Grunted like a pig and began undressing, expecting me to do the same. He tossed a nightgown at me. " Now hurry up" he said gruffly. Had he never been taught any manners? But I did feel faint and sleepy now and I knew my cotenant was trying to claim her body again. Well if I had to crawl into bed with this disagreeable man I would give it to her without a fight. I left into whatever place I usually went to and didn't wake up until the child inside had been born in January.

Nancy provides the most comprehensive history of the early childhood of Bernice from the time when the real Nancy went home after her visit for the summer until Bernas was sent to Birmingham. Her account confirms the fragmented information provided by the personalities for this period of time. Nancy did not have the amnesia that fragmented, the memories of the others. This is one of her accounts of memories.

It is not easy to be a person sharing a body with other entities, especially if you are not in communication with them. It is certainly no fun to be the one on the inside looking out. It is not so great for the one outside either if they are aware of the struggle inside.

I could not ask for a more beautiful, birthplace than the one where Bernas grew up. The natural fragrance of honeysuckle vines filled the open fields. The vivid freshness of tall pine trees and low growing cedar evergreens. I enjoyed the paradise of the woods, not unlike Eden. Bernas tasted a forbidden fruit, of creation within her own mind. More than she could cope with in later years. I know that my earliest memories went something like this. I would be aware of a conversation with my young friend who was perhaps six years old. We talked and argued as all children do, and gradually I would find myself in a world of breathing the wonderful fresh air of existence! Bernas would be gone, where I did not know or particularly care for the moment. I had life for the time being, That was all I asked for. It was wonderful to live to feel with one's own hands the smooth pebbles of a mountain stream to watch birds nesting, or peek at the young birds inside the nests. It was fun to watch as lizards scurried across scorching hot rocks in summer, to watch a lazy Blacksnake curled around low hanging branches, to come as close as possible and still be out of reach of a copperhead snake. I knew it was poisonous, but beautiful beyond description. It's rusty brown skin blotched and blending harmoniously patterned with the dry leaves surrounding it. It was also fun to go into the home with a small kitchen and big dining room to eat hot biscuits and fresh homemade butter with honey from the hives behind a barn, to be in front of the fireplace in winter. It was a great fireplace, the huge hearth. I remembered always that I did not belong in this house. This was Bernas Ruth's home and I was her guest. The people inside were her people, her papa, her sisters and brothers, and eventually her stepmother. I did not try to usurp her place with them. If Papa came to sit in front of the fire after his days work was finished , he would motion for Bernas to come and sit on his lap. I might wonder how it would be to sit on his lap and rub my hands over his face. and maybe pull his ears, but I did not do these things because Bernas treasured these times and she would climb onto his lap as quietly as a mouse sit there as still as a small rabbit waiting for danger to pass. Papa called her a good little girl and she was. Bernas also had times of deep remorse, and she would sit on the big rock, where we played happily at times that she would think of grievances when she had been offended by someone and this could happen very easily. She would retreat to a quiet place and cry silently. One place of retreat was a surprising place in view of our many fears. She would go under the high front veranda, typical of the southern made houses with lattice underpinning and high enough off the ground for a child to walk under . It was semi dark under the front porch, as we would call it today. No one would have thought to look for her there because she was definitely afraid of the dark. She would sit where angels fear to tread in a perfect retreat from crawling things and think of the things she would do when she grew up. She would think and tell me how she would go far away into the big city. She would be a very fine lady, and they would be sorry. It was not so much that she felt rejected as that she felt unequal , unable ,to stand up and talk back but the desire to do so was definitely there. There were times when she became so bold that I held back and wouid not match her adventuresome spirit. She was afraid of darkness to the extent of demanding a low burning light in her room at night.

There was a huge and craggy, lichen and moss covered sandstone rock with many tunnels and holes through it. The highest peak was easily 15 feet high. The rock was used as many things. A playhouse, a city school, but mostly it was a headquarters for starting the day for sitting hours on end watching nature operate, thinking and conversing together. Hanging over Bernas' arm almost a part of the child itself was usually the doll. Margaret Ann, She was a large doll.. Bernas pretended she was real, and she talked to her and conscientiously cared for her. The dolls were a source of dissension between the brothers and a sister. They were all for getting rid of the beat up old doll. Her oldest brother, Taylor, came armed with a package containing a doll. It was all dressed in pink and white shoes and yellow hair. It was a fascinating new toy and, was named Lucy Kathryn and placed on the mantel and was certainly no substitute for Margaret Ann. She was just a doll. But Margaret Ann lived and breathed and the embattled scars she suffered were compensated for by the fact that she was elevated to the status a human being in the eyes and mind of one person at least.

There was an uneasy tension in the house, often. The tension associated with papa's relationship with a certain local preacher's wife named Gertie. Aunts and uncles, and even the preacher himself came to the house and talked to Poppa about it. Popa sent them all away in a rage and dammed the whole world if they didn't stay out of this business. The older boys left home because of it. An older sister married because, as she said, she would not live in the same house with ", that woman" who moved in with her two daughters. Papa spent most of his time with her and had little time for Burnas and Bernas stayed on the big rock almost all the time now, coming to the house only when the calling became so insistent that she dared not disobey. She moved very quietly as if she was afraid she might be picked up bodily and thrown out of the house. A deep loneliness and fear lived within her. She cautioned me to be very quiet in the house. I could no longer eat at the table as the woman had said Papa had spoiled Bernas and she must not do such things as have two plates at the table. Margaret Ann was in danger also for the woman thought the old doll should be burned and one of the other dolls should be used for play instead. Bernas took Margaret Ann to the big rock and hid her there. Bernas ate very little. She mostly picked at her food while Papa scolded her and tried to force her to eat. The woman said he should take her to the doctor as her throat was obviously too sore because she could hardly swallow food.. But Bernas felt that if I could not eat then she should not be offered such privileges. so we ate together from the abundance of fruits and vegetables that grew on the farm. The woman pointed out over and over again that Bernas should be sent to live with her sister in Birmingham away from the only place that had been home and security and safety. Finally , one day Papa called Bernas to him and said she would be going to live with her sister. There would be a fine new school there would be new and delightful things, There would be a new baby Bernas could help take care of.

She screamed hysterically and long and when the screaming stopped she slept until morning.

The decision was finally and irrevocably arrived at. Bernas was to go away.

Well-meaning people planned the move believing it to be in the best interest of the child. She was like a shadow now. She was a ghostly creature that moved about in silence. To the adults her not eating and her sadness must have been proof that she needed a change of environment. To the child, it was a reaction to what amounted to the ultimate rejection of herself as a human being. It was proof of the unlovely features, such as the too large eyes and uncurly hair, and a totally useless and worthless, one. As if she were fit only to discard, to send away. We languished in the woods most of the time for the next few days. It was autumn and the chill of the early morning lingered and the leaves fell to the ground. The noises out of the outdoors changed. The crickets no longer sang. The fireflies diminished their lamps and no longer flickered like hundreds of neon lights. Bernas Ruth felt a vast sadness within and I picked up the mood. It was not easy to laugh and be happy. She explained to me that she could not play with me much longer. I did not feel gay at being with her as she told all the cows goodbye. She waited in the pasture in the evening waiting for the doctor but he did not come. Perhaps he was away. At any rate, she could not tell him goodbye. On the last morning, we huddled on the big rock together as long as we could and finally the voice called us. Barnas Ruth gathered Margaret Ann Held her close and sang a last lullaby to her. She kissed her battered and worn old face and then with the hoe she had brought for the purpose she swung the blade and severed the head . Sobbing with great painful sobs she said over and over "it's for your own good, Margaet Ann , it is for your own good." And then she pushed her up in the hollow scraped out place by the rock and covered her with leaves and needles from the great pine trees that we would see no more.

I did not go with her. I don't know where I went when the new black car came for her, She screamed and cried and pleaded to be left at home. But Papa kept saying, "It is for your own good, Bernas Ruth.It is for your own good" and she kicked and screamed as she was deposited bodily in the car. Suddenly the crying ceased and a strange and deep silence filled the air. She had her face in the crook of her arm and curled into a heap on the back seat of the car. There was a terrible hollow quietness inside like resolve never to cry again . Perhaps she felt it was no use. She went deeper inside and sensed only the shell of what was a little girl around me. I could not bear the desolate empty feeling, so I too slipped away though I do not know where I went.

Nancy wrote in a letter, of her memory of being at the home with Bernas. She wrote: " Let me begin at the beginning. This is just more or less theory, but it's probably accurate enough to be considered as a real explanation. There was a time I (Nancy) can remember very distinctly when a child called Bernas, or Bernas Ruth to be exact, and I were together. It was an odd sort of existence to be sure but a very satisfactory one, at least as far as I was concerned, it was okay. I had no mother (now I know that isn't possible) . I neither had nor wanted one. Papa was my father just as much as he was Bernas' father. He called me by my first name and her by hers. Thinking now, from an adult level, I think it must have been a game to papa but it was no game to us. He was a very good daddy, very indulgent. He was always bringing home gifts. Because he did not always bring me something she would cry sometimes or divide it if possible or give it to me. If I didn't have one, she didn't want one, either. Like the little blue silk umbrella he gave her. She would not open it until he brought one for me. Mine was red. She was unselfish and sympathetic. She would take things as a big production. When the time came that he decided to send her to Birmingham, since they made no decision about me, I didn't go anywhere. Bernas cried for days. She stayed out on the big rock, even took her clothes out there and wanted to just live there. She had it all figured out how to survive. I got left out of things. I don't know just how. I thought I was staying there with Papa. I visited once or twice in Birmingham and once or twice in Wyoming. It wasn't much of a visit because she was different again. We could not play or even talk much. I don't know what happened for years and years. I pieced some things together second hand, and sometimes it's like a memory . When I began to be aware of things again, it was almost unbelievable, what had happened. She lived here. She or so I thought it was she, Bernas, or was it Bernice, was married and pregnant. Try to think how I felt suddenly you are sort of pregnant. Yet you're not. It's funny isn't it? It was an awareness, an observing. She had bad teeth and a toothache but I didn't feel any pain and I didn't have bad teeth. She had headaches backaches dizzy spells, she was a nervous wreck. I had no wish to step into those shoes. The only thing I wanted to do was to help out. I read a great deal and it occurred to me that what we did need was a psychiatrist. I have realized for some time that we're separate identities. I was afraid you would never catch on, and I could not get free to tell you. I had a hard time forcing this mind and body to see you. I don't agree with you on the voluntary basis here, because someone always volunteers to quit. And I say no, not till some sort of adjustment is made. It took me too long to get this far to risk losing things. I have had to change, and give up several ideas I had and I'm none the worse for it. In fact, I am not sure that I have enough wisdom to handle things alone. There was a time when my only thought was to be free just for the sake of being free and now I have come to realize that I can't just be free. I have to have a good perspective and outlook, even a purpose. Life isn't that simple. My purpose is to help Bernice get better by continuing to get your help."

I confirmed to Nancy that this was a good purpose and I appreciated her assistance and her providing helpful information about past and present observations.

I then focused on Bernice's complaint.

I asked Bernice to listen and then I said:"The little girl is the source of feeling lonely and empty. She longs for her home. It is going to take time for her to become comfortable in your home. When she is comfortable, you will feel much more comfortable too and there will be one less trouble in Bernas' load on her back. Let me talk to her and see if I can help her understand her new situation. If you are willing to do that, please close your eyes and let me count you down to the beach. You have closed your eyes so now I will count for you to go down the steps. Going down now, 10 to 9,8, 7, 6, 5, 4, 3, 2, 1, and sit down and look at the ocean waves. I want to talk to the little girl, who was hiding behind a rock. I am your doctor now. I want to help you. Can you hear me?

"Yes."

"I want to tell you what has happened. When your Papa came to get you to put you in the car, you were able to stop feeling anything outside. It was like you were able to turn off feeling your body, and you did not know that he took your body and put it in the car and you thought you were still hiding behind a rock. When I asked you to wake up, you woke up here in my office. I want you to wake up here again now and let me talk with you. Good , You are awake now. Look at me and see that I am real. You can see I am not a dream. Look around at my office. You are really here now. I want you to look at your hands and feel them. They are much larger. Feel your body. Your body has been growing while you were sleeping. Your body is a grown-up body now, and you are in it with grown-up people in your mind with you. One of the grown-up people with you in your mind is Bernice. She controls the body now and when you leave she will take you in the body to her home, which will be your home too now. I want you to learn to be at home in this new home. Another grown-up person in this body with you is Nancy. I have asked her to be your friend and talk with you and help you. I also want Bernice to get to know you and help you to feel at home in her home which will be your home too. Many years have passed since you went to sleep, and much has changed since then. I know it will feel strange, and it will take time for, you to get used to the changes. There are six children now in the home with Bernice and Nancy and you'll get to know them and their names and they can be your friends and playmates. I know that you're going to be sad because you can't go back to your old home right now. I'm very sorry about that, but many years have passed since you went to sleep in this body. Your body has been moved to a city that is far away from your home that you used to have. It will not do any good to keep saying: "I want to go home", because no one can take you there now. So I would like you to stop saying I want to go home and to learn to be in this home with Bernice, Nancy and the children. I want Nancy to talk to you now and to tell you that she will help you feel at home in this new home. "

"Nancy!, I want you to become aware now of being with the little girl, who will be going home with you and is going to feel sad because she misses her home. Please tell her you will be her friend, and you will help her feel at home in this new home. I will pause a few minutes to let you have time to talk to her."

Pause

"Now that you have had time to do that, I would like to talk to Bernice again."

"Bernice!, you can wake up now as I count from one to three. Waking up now, one two three, wake up now."

"Bernice, I have talked to the little girl and I have explained to her, her situation and have asked Nancy to help take care of her and I also explained to her that you will be with her too. I hope you can get to know her and talk to her and help her feel at home in your home. In the last visit, I helped Bernas with some things that I hope will help her feel better and I had hoped to tell you about that at this time, but we have run out of time. We can talk about it the next time I see you. I have asked the little girl to stop saying' I want to go home.' I hope she will be able to do that and not disturb you. Feel free to call me if you need me. Goodbye."

Bernice called saying the child was very annoying and I consulted with Nancy about management of her. Nancy promised she would take her home when she could and told her to go back to sleep and that she would wake her up when the time came to take her home.

When Bernice came for her next appointment, I told her: "I am very sorry the little girl disturbed you so much. When you called me, I asked Nancy to talk to her and tell her that she's with her and will help take care of her. I hope this helped with her. I made a mistake, because I should have waited until I had more time to work with her. I should have realized that the reason she got in this situation she was in was because she did not want to leave home and that she would be quite disturbed to find out she was not at home yet. Now I will have time to talk to her again and will explain to her the new situation and encourage her to accept her new home with you."

"I do not know what you are doing. Is this something you are suggesting?"

"I am focusing my attention on both sources of distress and reprogramming your mind to become comfortable in the present time. For example, this child hid behind a rock to prevent her father from putting her in a car and sending her with her sister to Birmingham. When her father found her she dissociated by turning off her awareness of what was happening outside and has been suspended in time for all these years since then. She is the source of some of the distress that Bernas is experiencing represented by the large bag of burdens on her back. This child is a source of feelings of fear and abandonment. She feels sadness and loneliness. By dissociating to avoid being taken from her home, she has become stranded in time. She needs to be brought back to life in this time and helped to accept her present situation and to grow up. She represents just one part of the work I did with Bernas during your last visit.

I also have worked with Bernas about her feelings of being unlovable. I helped her correct her beliefs that she was not worth caring about. She thought that if she were good enough, her mother would not have died. She also felt that if she was good enough her father would not have sent her away with her sister to Birmingham. She also believed she was unacceptable, because her brother-in-law called her a no good snotty nosed stupid girl. I told her these beliefs were not true and that she is a good girl and is lovable and she can believe that people will love her. I believe this will help Bernas change her beliefs about herself and she will feel acceptable and worthy. You have been amnesic for about the first seven years of your life. Some very devastating things happened to you during that time. Your mind has used amnesia to spare you the bad memories and emotions from these experiences so that you could survive them. They are represented by the 'troubles on Bernas' back. Telling you this is called' interpretation', but telling you is not enough. The beliefs have to be resolved where they are held in your mind before you can be mentally healthy there. There is no way to resolve them without your feeling the pain that is there before it is relieved .The pain is there for a good purpose. It tells me where you're hurting. I am sorry you have to feel it to get the help you need there.. It is your choice whether you want to feel your pain to get well there or to continue to feel your unresolved distress. What do you want to do?"

"That is a painful decision. I'll have to think about it."

"Since I have awakened the little girl and cannot put her back to sleep like she was, I would like to work with her to help her become comfortable in the present. If you would agree to that, close your eyes, and I will continue to work with her. I see you have closed your eyes. So I will count for you to go down the steps and sit and watch the beach. You will be going down now, while I count for you. 10 going down nine going down eight, seven , six, five, four, three, two, one. Now sit on the steps and enjoy watching the ocean"

" I want to speak to the little girl who was hiding behind a rock. Where you were hiding behind a rock, I want you to be able to hear me now. I am Dr. Young. I'm going to be your doctor. You are in my office now, and I want you to wake up here with me. Open your eyes and look around. Look at me. I want to tell you some things that you can learn about how you came to be here now. Your Papa found you behind the rock, but you stopped seeing and feeling your body, You believed you still were able to hide from him. You stopped knowing what was happening outside. You did not know that he put you in the car and sent you to Birmingham with your sister. Many years have passed since you started hiding. Your body has kept a growing and has grown up now. Do you remember me?"

"Yes, You are Dr. Young. I want to go home."

"I know you do. But the home you lived, is far away and there is no way to get you back there now. It has been many years, since you were there and I do not know if the house is still there, and if it is I don't know if anyone is still living there now. Until we can find out about that, you need to stay at the home that is near here. There are other people living in your body with you. They are grown-up people who have a home for you to live in and they will take care of you. They will love you and help you to feel at home, where they live now. I want you to listen to them, and you do what they ask you to do. I want you to stop saying. ' I want to go home', because they can't take you there. I'm sorry about that, but in time, you will be able to feel it home in this new home that they have for you. They have six children in the home, and I want you to meet them and learn to live with them and play with them. I will be seeing you again, and Bernice and Nancy will take you to their home now... Go back to sleep now, and I will ask Nancy to wake you up when she can talk with you. "

" Nancy!, I want you to listen. I have talked to the little girl and have told her that you will take her to her new home and that you'll wake her up when you have time to talk with her and I want you tell her information about the new home and the others living there. It will take her a while to get used to being in this new home, but she will eventually become at home there. She is going to be homesick for a while. I have asked her to stop saying she wants to go home, because you can't take her there. And I have asked her to do what you tell her to do. Call me if you need help. You can wake up now and take her home. You can be her foster mother. I appreciate how much you help. I'll see you next time."

When Bernice came in for her next visit, she had a seat and started talking.

"I have decided not to continue. I like to do things quickly and get them over with. I need more frequent visits."

"I know you do but your finances don't permit you to come more frequently. You have been writing to me between visits, and maybe we can do some of the work by correspondence. I want to read what you write and respond to it as I can. I received something from you in the mail, I wonder if you were aware of writing it. It is different from what you have been writing me before. The little girl is called an idiot and Nancy is called a fool. Are you aware writing it? "(I showed her the letter.)

"No I didn't write it and don't know anything about it."

Her eyes closed, and then reopened. She had a new look, which was confident and she spoke with a self-assured and somewhat harsh tone. "I wrote that. I am tired of this utter nonsense. It has to be stopped."

"I understand your frustration with it and understand your wish to change it. It comes from parts of your mind, and there is no way to get rid of these parts of your mind. One solution is to repress them, but that will take your energy to keep them imprisoned and you also lose the potential value that they can have. The solution is to accept them and work to change what can be changed for the better."

"I think they are useless not worth the bother."

"You sound like your brother-in-law, Mary Lou's husband. He called Bernas, a good for nothing snotty nosed idiot."

"He was right she should be gotten rid of too."

"You are in a role of being a persecutor or a villain. You have a lot of strength and confidence and you can become very helpful and constructive. I hope you can join me in getting this mind straightened out. It may be hard for you to believe that much good can come from your mind. I hope you will join me and other parts of your mind in making that happen."

"Pardon me, but maybe you're a fool too."

"Well, I'm sure you will be watching me and I hope to demonstrate to you that good changes can be made. Do you have a name for yourself?

"I am Anne"

"I am glad to meet you Anne. If you write me, you can sign your name as BA or introduce yourself as Anne so I will know who you are..I invite you to join me and some of the rest of your mind in straightening out the chaos in your mind. We can do it if we work together. Think about it. Thanks for talking with me. Now, let me talk to Nancy."

" Nancy!, please talk with me. How are you and the little girl getting along?"

"She is getting better. She is not so homesick and she is feeling more at home with us. I am enjoying being like her mother."

"Thanks for taking care of her. You do a good job. I promised to speak to her again and I would like to talk with her now. So, until the next time, goodbye for now. "

" I want to talk to the little girl that was behind the rock. Little girl, come wake up and talk with me. Nancy tells me you are feeling more at home in your new home. You are getting over your sadness about missing your old home. We call it homesickness, and you will gradually get over it. You will be growing up soon and I want to give you a name, because you will not always be a little girl. Since you were hiding behind a rock, I thought we might call you Roxanne. I hope that is okay with you, if it is tell Nancy I gave you the name and your name is now Roxanne. When I will talk with you again, I will call for you by saying I want to speak to Roxanne. Did you get my Christmas card?"

"Yes, it has three camels and a star on it. I can write. I wrote you a thank you note. I will ask Nancy to send it to you."

"I'm very proud of you. You are doing really good. I will talk to you again next time. You are learning to like your new home, and the people living with you there. Keep on being very good. I will talk to you again next time. Goodbye."

"Bernice! You can wake up now, when I count to three. Waking up now, one two three. Welcome back. I hope you enjoyed your visit to the seashore."

"Yes, it was very refreshing and relaxing."

"I hope you can use the routine of going down the steps to the seashore. When you want to go to sleep or take a break for a while, you can take a trip to the seashore whenever you choose. I talked to your mind that wrote the note to me and she gave her the name as Anne. She reminds me of your brother- in- law who was so critical. I hope she can change to be more positive. I think she will. She has a lot of potential to become a very important and helpful part of your mind. You'll be surprised how much your mind can become able to help you. You have a very good mind. It has just been broken to pieces ,taken apart, but can be put back together again. Humpty Dumpty is not impossible. I know it is very frightening to have someone tinkering with your mind. It is frightening to have someone operating on your body but it is more frightening when it is your mind. I will try to keep you informed about what I'm doing. I established a relationship with Anne and encouraged the little girl in her progress in adjusting to her new home. Since I expect her to grow up in time, I gave her the name of Roxanne, which I chose because she was hiding behind a rock. So, from now on, she will be known as Roxanne. I will have to go slow until Roxanne adjusts to her new home. I have learned that there is another child hiding under the porch from Papa. She feels cold and hungry. I think her symptom of feeling hungry is resulting in your raiding the refrigerator and makes it hard for you control your weight. We will correct that when we can get to her. I also need to spend more time with Bernas. I want to assure you that all of this is your mind and was in your unconscious .It will become conscious to you in time and restore your whole mind to consciousness."

"Well, I hope you know what you're doing . You are right in that it does frighten me. I will see you next time."

Bernice canceled her appointments and I did not see her for months Then the following letter came in the mail along with a transcription of three tapes.

"Dear Dr., Anne says that you said that she was a villain and she is very angry at you. She won't come back. She made an appointment to see Dr. H.. I have enclosed the transcription of three tapes."

On the tapes, Anne said I was a fool and asked for help in getting rid of the other occupants of her body. Although she is not identified as Bernas, I'm sure Bernas told her about her playmates, including Nancy and Anne. She said Anne had been bossy and, wanted to always have her way and the others did not like to play with her. Dr. H. told Anne that the others had a right to be in the body and Anne could go invade somebody else's body

46

like she was a spirit if she wanted to. Anne said Dr. H. was a fool if she thought Anne could just go into anybody's body that she chose. So, Anne was not pleased with Dr. H but Bernice was because Dr. H. made house calls called on the telephone frequently and was very supportive.

Other letters that came in the mail were as follows:

"Dear Dr. sometimes it seemed like a losing battle. I'm so tired of having to fight and struggle through every day. I'm so tired putting all my effort into a day and results of being (an incomplete sentence).

Dr. I'm tired. I'm tired. There's no end to the tension and stress. It's such a false front. I don't feel good, and there's not really a person on earth to turn to. They all think I'm so capable. Why must I always be the strong one. I am tired and I can't rest. I really am not lovable. I can't be accepted by anyone I'm so different. Must I live just for the kids always? There is no meaning to life. I'll never be well. It is just a hope, but not really true. What a false front, the dressing up and getting hair done and running around the office like a business woman. And pretending to be so capable and being admired. Doctor she wants to hide me and not let me be seen by these new people and know that I exist. But I do exist, and I'm no good. I'm sick doctor, and I'm tired. But I want to be loved too and not be different. I'm afraid, but mostly, I don't care. Bernas.

Another letter.

Dear Dr. there's nothing you can do for me. She's very sick again. I think sometimes she will destroy us all. No man could have been more considerate and kind than Keith, and I respected him so much. Sure he had his faults, and he loves to manipulate people, but he also had so many good points. This place I woke up in(11:30 p.m.) is such a dump. How any person could take three children here. I long for Keith, and his contented snoring, but I also know he is proud and well disciplined, and it would not be useful if I went back and tried to explain. I wish I could change into a normal person. I have to become more stable or I will surely die trying.. Keith will be so bitter and well he might be. He tried very hard. Will I find my way to tell Keith he must not be bitter. He can find a more decent person, and he deserves better. I am afraid of love.(Bernice.added to this:" Who wrote this note.?") I must not Live. I Spoil Things. I Am Most Wicked and Bad, No Life Force Very Bad Pig like Me. I was a bother to Him. He Is Better off without Me. I Love Him. No more men.)

On the third page was the following:

Dear Dr. young.

Well, we have gotten ourselves in another mess. I don't know if there's a way out or not. If this episode ends our marriage to Keith then we've had it. I suppose.

In short: Bernas felt unwanted and a bother to Keith (ridiculous!). She felt there was unfair housework and she wasn't able to keep up Keith's immaculate standards.(He is too fanatic about order and work is above all other virtues). So, she recently rented a very old house at the end of a muddy lane in Orangevale and took things up there in the station wagon without letting him know. And she made arrangements for a truck to come and move the furniture. We have to hear. I don't know what to do ,to go up and get the things or to tell Keith or what – dammit all! Keith has been the sole of goodness. I am disgusted. I wish I could talk to you.

A note came from Roxanne .It was written in a red ink and cramped small print .It slanted up to the right on the page and looked distressed and not up to her previous improving printing.

Dear Dr.

I am tired of being a big girl. I want my father. I want Keith because I have no one and I cannot sleep at all. Why does not Keith come for me and take me home? I hurt inside, because I have no father. What is the matter with me that no one loves me? I think it is not much too good to be just alone.. I love everybody, but no one loves me, and it is not fair. I want Keith and I do not want any more time to pass because if I wake up I know he is gone. Please get help

.

This typed letter followed about two days later.

Dear Zo,

I thought Id better send along a word of cheer to let you know that Roxanne got over her fit of loneliness and self-pity. We really had a bout with depression for about 48 hours, but it subsided as usual

Loneliness and the need to have someone to love and be loved by is a big part to trigger these depressed moods. I am sure. But, again, I maintain that Keith is not the answer. He does not even deserve us. We must take our time… Eventually, a worthwhile person will come into our lives. I have so much to be thankful for in our friend Danny. There is no romance left… This was just a quick flame that I extinguished because I have no intention of being someones mistress... Even someone as nice as Danny. He was very angry and swore we would never see him again, but he could not stand of all things a promiscuous one or a "coal-assed"(Lithuanian accent made it sound so amusing) woman.. But compared to a promiscuous one, a coal-assed woman was far worse of the two evils... He was terribly disappointed in me because he never had me figured for a coal-assed woman. This was several months ago, and finally, he said okay then.. Be that as it may, we have a very good platonic relationship. Something that is special because we ask nothing of each other... Just mutual friendship. As he says," a sort of spiritual relative" sort of thing. Anyway, he visits us several times a week, amuses the little kids for hours with tales of his travels... And genuinely appreciates being around. I think this is far more viable. Right now while we are getting a foundation with ourselves, Myself empresses it is better than getting all involved in a romance which would mean Roxanne would have someone to keep her covered up at night. So,I now must go to bed. It is 11 p.m.. I just want to tell you that things settled down.. We are very happy and doing fine again even Roxanne. Sincerely., Bernice.

Bernice came into the office and handed me three neatly written pages, which follow:

Dear Dr.

I am going to try and describe what just happened to me.

I woke about 7:45, and all was quiet, so I thought it would be a good time to go over the material you had given me. You know ,the carbons. Believe it -- I've tried a hundred times to read them. And every time I read a page or two, I get weak ,dizzy and sort of fade out. Something happens. When I try to write, either material for you or for any other purpose this happens too. I think nice things and feel inspired and eager and then I start to become vague, sleepy and dizzy and become so weak I crawl into bed and linger in sort of limbo. I am In between life and sleep.

This is also what happens when I work in public -- or when I tried to participate in activities of any sort. But to sit around the house or to go on necessary shopping and routine -- a limited routine, at that I can proceed. But with any constructive or creative effort or ambition -- mostly ambition and opportunities to be effective in a part of the tree of life, I get these unreasonable fears and weak trembles and have to retreat. People can 't understand it and neither can I. It is what held me back this morning. I was eager for spending the whole morning writing -- I suddenly began getting dizzy and weak and I thought resistant. As I always do, I passed out for not very long perhaps 15 minutes to an hour and then as I came back, very slowly, I was so weak and still am, very weak, and I literally crawled to the bed and dragged myself in, and I called you. What frightens me so is the message on the attached pages. This being rendered helpless happens often enough that I know I will gradually regain myself. Usually, I sleep for awhile and wake refreshed to a degree.

It seems I have some part that deliberately does this to me, and it is ruining my life. I have been pushed around and I have catered to it long enough. I don't know how, but I think it is time for reckoning with it. Time for a showdown, shall we say. I have made myself almost a semi-invalid for years trying to keep this part satisfied -- and I either have to give in for the rest of my life and spend half of it in bed or find a cure and subdue whatever or whoever it is that wrote this nasty letter. I just don't think I should be rendered useless by some unconscious force that can become dominant over me. I do have potential, and this part thinks I should remain in a closed room! This is exactly what I have done for years. At least half of the time, and I've compromised and spent about as much of the daytime hours in bed as a up and around, and it is not right. I feel like I have either to change this or die trying. It's not right to be a half a person -- please help me -- help me and find this one who writes this. And if we have to use force to deal with her, then we will -- it just has to be seen about. If we can deal with it and straighten it out, I know I can be normal and happy and effective in life. I don't know who wrote this. It isn't Bernas or any others I know. The only clue I can offer is that I was reading the part where you talked to the conscience. That is when I started feeling weak and dizzy, and maybe it is that one".

Bernice handed me five pages torn from a secretary's notebook.

"Young -- you gave her pills again to make her not feel so much. I hope she dies and I hate her so much. She is a crazy old thing. Why do you not stop and let me kill her. Slowly. I just don't like her. There's nothing good in her at all. I want her dead, dead, dead. Don't you see what I mean, she is miserable, and I want her helpless and sleeping. I want her never moving or always running around trying to be a person. I can make her weak and dizzy and ache in her head and back and arms and legs and I can make her shake and be afraid and tremble. I don't like her at all. I hate her and her god damn trying to live. I intend she shall die. I definitely intend to see her die. I want her behind a closed door and hidden. I want her smothered and choked to death. I want her sick in a dark room. I want her away from all beauty. She is evil and must not be happy. Make her crazy and sick, like me. I am not too live. She must also die. She must not have help and she must not work and dress in pretty clothes. She must not comb her hair or have comfort. She can have only a long night gown with lots of cover and never get out of bed. I hate her wanting to make trouble for me and dragging me out of bed. I'm sick, and I want darkness -- put her in a prison and I won't kill her -- make sure she is locked inside a room with just a place to lie down and cover up and don't let her have any food -- maybe old bread and a little water. She has to stop this thinking that she can be in nice places. I won't stand for it. She can't write a book and I won't let her be so stuck up and thinking she can do something smart. She is crazy like me. now you listen to me and send her where crazy people are and I won't kill her. I will not make her die if she suffers like I do. She has to be sick too. She has to be hateful and repulsive and not good and kind. She must not have friends to love her, no one loves me. So she can't have love too. Now you quit trying to help her -- I can't make you give up like I make everyone else give up. Why don't you give up too and let her die. You try to help a crazy old fool. -- she is. I insist she be a crazy old fool like me. I am not to be pulled out into places where people can see me. It's a dire state of the dark place. And she has to stay there too. How would you like to be a hateful mean person and have to see people loving her and hating you? Now it's not fair to me. She can be crazy too. She thinks she can do everything. She can't cause I won't let her. Make her stay in her place. She is a servant and a prisoner and she deserves to be punished for trying to drag me out. I will kill her before she keeps pushing me out for people to see. You had better stop trying to help her or I will make her take all the pills in the house or I will make her take a sharp knife and cut her head off or drive us into the river. She is a tragedy trying to be something she isn't. I hate her"

I said: "Bernice, this one must be a child, who believes she has done something very wrong and she feels ashamed and guilty and ashamed to be seen. I think if she can be forgiven and her self-esteem restored she can feel like living and let you live too. I think she is behind Bernas and strongly influences what Bernas feels Let's find out what is bothering her. Close your eyes and I will count you down to the beach. Going down now one step at a time when I count for you. 10 nine, eight, seven, 6, 5, 4, 3, 2, 1, sit down and enjoy looking at the waves of the ocean."

"Somewhere in your mind, you wrote this note to me, saying you wanted me to stop helping her. Please come out here and talk to me."

She covered her face with her hands and seemed to shrink back in the chair. I asked her why she felt so bad.

Her face became grotesque. Her veins became engorged. Her body stiffened. She looked extremely agitated. I said: "I can see that you feel horrible. What has happened?

"I killed three children."

This shocked me . I calmed myself and asked :

"How old are you?"

"Seven".

"what is your name?

"Ruth"

"What were their names?"

"Margaret Anne, Jane, and Patty Jo."

"Were these your dolls?"

"Yes, but they talked to me."

.

"Why did you kill them?"

"Papa was going to send me away and he would not let me take them with me. I could not leave them alone. It would be worse than dying to have no mother. It was better to kill them than to leave them alone. So, I took them out under the cedar tree behind the house and chopped off their heads and buried them. I am so very ashamed that I killed them. But I felt I had to do it. I could not leave them without a mother"

"That they talked to you, tells me that they were in your mind because dolls cannot really talk to you and the talk comes from your mind that talks for the dolls. So, they are really alive but in your mind and not in the dolls. So I know that you did not kill them in the dolls. So, they are still alive in your mind. I can awaken them, and you can join up again. I will talk to them now. Margaret Anne, you can hear me. I am Dr. Young, and I'm here with you and I will protect you and you are safe now. I know you are still alive. Your mother did not kill you. She did not want to kill you. She did not know that she could take you with herself inside her head. Her mother had died and she knew how terrible it feels to be a child with- out a mother and she did not want you to suffer like that and thought you would be better off dead which means she loves you very much and she is going to be very happy you are still alive and can be together again. Come out and be with me.

The eyes opened and there was a sudden look of terror. She leaped from the chair and ran under the desk. I leaned down and asked:

"Why are you hiding?"

"She's going to kill me."

"Listen to what I have to tell you. Her Papa was going to send her to Birmingham with her sister and your stepmother told him not to let her take you dolls with her because it was crazy for her to think the dolls could talk to her which you really could. The mean old witch did not know that you could talk to her and it is real and not crazy. You really could talk to Ruth inside her mind. So, your little mother believed that you would be better off dead than to have to be alone without a mother. That is because her mother had died and she knew how painful that was to be without a mother. So, she thought if she killed and buried you she would save you from awful loneliness. But you really were in her mind all the time and not in the dolls. That is why you are still alive and able to talk to me. She does not want to kill you. She wants to be with you and misses you very much. She has felt very sad and bad, because she believed she had killed you and has believed what she did was unforgivable. She will be glad that you and Patty Jo and Jane are still alive and you can all be together again. I am going to tell her to talk to all of you and you can all talk to her again, and you can all be happy together. She loves you and will be very very glad you are still alive and you can be with her again. I want you all to feel safe with her now. "

"You all will have a period of time to talk to each other now."

After five minutes, I asked her "Ruth, did you get get back together again?
"

"Yes, doctor, we're all happy together now."

"Ruth, you do not have to feel guilty anymore. You did not really kill them and what you did do was out of loving kindness to protect them from the pain you have gone through because you lost your mother. You did what you did for good reasons. You are forgiven for what you did. You're not bad. You did what you believed was right and you had good reason to believe that what you did was right. You are forgiven. You do not have to feel guilty anymore. You are not guilty.
"

"Are you God?"

"No, but I am a wise doctor and I can forgive you and I do forgive you. You do not have to feel ashamed or have to hide anymore. You are a good person, and you have the right to happiness so you can be happy now and let Bernice be happy too. You have been thinking that you are bad and unworthy for so long, that it may have become a habit to feel you are bad so you will need to keep reminding yourself that you have been forgiven and you are worthy of love and acceptance and happiness. If you slip back into the old way of thinking remember to remind yourself that you have a new way of thinking about yourself now. My words of understanding will be with you always and you may hear them whenever you need them. Now take these memories with you and let me speak to Bernice again. Bernice!, you can wake up and come back from the beach now. Wake up as I count to three. Waking up now, 1, 2, 3, wake up now. The personality that wrote the angry things is named Ruth. When her father was going to send her to Birmingham with your sister, he would not let her take three dolls with her. I suspect it was the stepmother's idea not to let her have the dolls, and it was also her idea to send you to Birmingham in the first place .This self is named Ruth, She believed her dolls were alive because in her mind she was able to talk with them and they talked to her. Since she had lost her own mother and knew how unhappy she was after her mother's death, she believed it would be merciful to kill the dolls rather than leave them without a mother. So, she took them out behind the house under a cedar tree, chopped off their heads and buried them. She believed she had killed her three children and felt extremely sad and guilty. The children were really in her mind and not in the outside dolls. I was able to reunite them and to give Ruth forgiveness. I have told her she is worthy of love and acceptance and happiness, and that she can be happy now and let you be happy too. If you can communicate to her by thought or on paper you can encourage her to feel that she is okay now. She needs your acceptance and love. Welcome her to join you in living. I hope this will help stop the sabotaging that was coming from her. She has been the source of some of the miserable feelings you have had and I expect you are going to feel much better now. This self can become a source of much positive strength if all of yourself will accept and nourish her. I will look forward to your your next visit."

I received in the mail the following letter from Ruth. It was signed Ruth and her maiden name:

Dear Dr. Young,

I have come into the world to live with the rest of me. I can't say I like it too well, but what must be done must be done. I cannot stay hidden inside these layers of fat. So I will have to see them removed. I have to learn to live with the rest of me. I may make mistakes, but they will help. As I write this I am afraid, but you cannot help me to not be afraid. I do not know what we can do for a living. I know we are an adult with children, and therefore must work. I am sorry, but I will have to dismiss your services. I will need friends, and you may be my friend if you want, but a doctor I neither need or can afford. I will not come for visits to your office as you must work for a living too. I'm not sick, but just need to think better. I will learn to believe I can be like other people, but you cannot help me to learn this as I have already told you once, I will not buy a friend and I am not sick, just beginning to live. I will not buy love, as it is to be given of its own free will. It is only real if it is given. Now, you must trust me to learn to live and not tell me I must not come back to talk to you. If you want to talk to me, you may visit my home as a friend should, if not a friend, you are of no value to me. I buy your time no more.

If I try I can make it and I will try. I have to try. I have some children. They go to school and require many things. I watched them in the high school parade. I didn't have these experiences, so I'm happy to see them. They are not sick. They can compete in the world. One girl is head cheerleader and led the band down the street just looking pretty. Another girl helped make a float and rode in it and had a costume. The boy drove the Jeep covered with paper and full with boys. The little ones watched and said they would do these things too some day and they will.

I think I have some friends, though I do not know yet which ones I can trust so I do not depend on any one yet. We will work and if we get fired, then we will just get another job. We have to.

I'm not sure I can say I like living, but I am going to learn to like it if I can. We have to live it seems because we have to raise these children. I would not want them to not have a mother. I hope my news does not disturb you that I can't use you anymore. I just don't want to spend my money for conversation. You said you could love me with a form of love. If you do then, whether I come there being sick has no bearing on the matter. Either one does, or one doesn't that's the way life is. We don't buy things except those things to remain alive. I cannot buy another person's encouragement. I had to buy a man's time to fix the car, and I understood that. The car cannot think and fix itself. I can think, so, I have to fix myself. If I had a broken arm, I would pay you to fix it. But now that I have come into the world, I don't use you for I'm not inside. Can you understand? Now, don't have your feelings hurt. I have to live and would not have pride if I came to you and paid you to hold my hand and tell me I could be like other people. I must try it and see if I can. I can because I have to. You will say, but I can help you enjoy being alive. But you can't. Either I learn to enjoy it or I don't. I need to love and be loved. I might find such a thing, but I cannot in this body. So I will change it to a smaller one by not eating so much food and I will save money too and I might buy me a pretty dress too. We have clothes that are all big, because we are big, but I don't think it is necessary to be so big. Now you don't worry about us. You may be our friend, but we cannot have you for a doctor. I have to go to work now. Thank you, your friend, Ruth.(She is only mildly over weight. She exaggerates the degree of her obesity).

I replied as follows:

Dear Ruth,

I received your letter, and I'm very glad that you decided to join in living. Perhaps I can be a friend who helps you like a coach who may assist you in learning to live. As you mention you have helpers inside, who can help you, and as a coach, I will offer suggestions that I hope will be helpful. I can do this by correspondence, which will not require office time and I will not charge you for it. This will be freely given. This is an example of the kind of love I can give freely. I have noticed in the things you have sent in the mail that some of your inner selves have been talking to each other by typing back and forth. Your selves can increase this ability to communicate with each other. They can also become able to communicate with disconnected selves that need to be made conscious and blended in with the rest of yourself, including you. So the suggestions are to all of you. Your self has observed what I've been doing. And so you have been learning how to do it. I start with some clue that there is a part that is giving an indication of a need for assistance. I like the proverb 'where there is smoke, there is fire'. Where there is distress there is a consciousness of the cause of the distress and you can ask the mind there what the cause is and search for and treat for a solution. For another example the mind may give clues such as in a dream. From a dream Nancy had I learned a child was hiding behind a rock to avoid Papa from sending her away. I also have gotten a clue that there is a child hiding under the porch. She feels she is starving and I think she is a source of the hunger that you are trying to fill with the over eating. I would suggest that at some time when you think the time is right, that one of your selves ask to talk to her as' the one hiding under the porch' and tell her she can come out now because Papa is no longer here and she is safe now. You would then need to orient her to the present circumstances. Just like Roxanne has been helped to become at home in the present. I have also had a note from someone who said that she has been a bad mother because she was afraid and kept the children hidden for safety. She needs help in overcoming her fearfulness and her over protectiveness to the children. A part of you that is unafraid such as Anne or Nancy may help her to be unafraid. The story that Nancy told Roxanne about mother Robin applies to this mother. This is what Roxanne wrote:

Dear Dr.

Once there was a mother Robin who had some little birds in her nest. She loved her little birds so much that she always stayed with them to keep care of them. It was night time, and there was no sun in the sky. Only very small stars and a half moon to give light. And when it was time for screech owls and whippoorwills to make night noises, she would stay awake to protect the little birds. In the daytime, she would stay even if big clouds came, even if it rained and thundered and lightened, even if the wind blew the tree until the nest almost felt out. The mother bird grew tired and sleepy. She turned pale and was not bright like other robins. And she could not be strong because she was not getting exercise. All was because she was afraid to leave the little birds. They could not learn to fly because she sat on them to keep them warm and to keep them safe from harm. All was because she was afraid. And because she was afraid the little birds could not see very often. The Robin was tired and afraid and kept sitting on them. They could often not get enough air. So they suffered from no air, and for light. The mother Robin did not at all intend for little birds to be unhappy. She thought they should be inside and be quiet so enemies would not attack them. Then somehow the old Robin grew so tired and weak that she could not sit on the nest day and night. So they began to get out. One time a little bird found a friend. This friend was a blue Jay, a big one, but he did not hurt the bird. So the young Robin took the old mother to see the blue Jay and he laughed at her fears. He said young robins must learn to fly, and that no one would hurt anyone else. Even mother Robin learned there were nice people, and nice birds. She let the young birds have air and light, and they soon learned to walk and even to fly and the mother did not have to work so hard either keeping them all in the nest. So, it was a very unnecessary thing to do, because of being afraid and no one should be afraid that way .Love, Roxanne.

This mothering self has gotten the message from Nancy's story and is ready to change. She needs acceptance and reassurance and assistance. She has apparently hidden children that she can help find and bring back to life. They can be sources of energy and joy in living. You can ensure safety for her and the children, some of whom she said are in the forest. She also told me she had created selves that she put up front to hide behind because she was too afraid to be seen and that they became automatons (had a will of their own and no longer under her control)(an interesting observation).

You have the ability to incorporate personalities into your mind, and you can incorporate me, if you choose to do so, that way, my voice will always go with you if you choose to hear it .You can have your own" Dr. Young" in your mind. You can think,' what would Dr. Young say' and what you think I would say will come to mind. You can choose whether it seems like a good idea are not. (Don't hold me responsible if it is not good advice, You are responsible if you choose to use it, Ha Ha). The suggestions you get will be from your own mind and you do not have to feel that I'm telling you what to do.

Also, I'm not trying to run your life in absentia.

I suggest that all of you become the sources of soothing and reassurance to yourself and you can touch yourself pleasantly. You can " pleasure" yourself. When we are born we have to depend on someone outside for soothing and pleasant touching. We come to expect this to come from outside but as we grow older we should become able to become the source within ourselves when we need soothing and loving. Thus, we do not have to forever remain dependent on others for this need and we can become less desperately dependent on others. Then, our relationships to others can become more relaxed and comfortable. This will relieve the desperation you have to be loved. You will be less a desperately needy person and to have self confidence, acceptance and love from inside and outside. Just as your body heals your physical wounds, your mind can heal your emotional wounds. You can love yourself. That is taken for granted in the instruction' Love your neighbor as your self'. You are to be able to love yourself first and then you can love your neighbor. As Ruth has said "how can you be happy when others are loved and you are not?" It helps if we are loved a lot in the early years of our lives and it is more difficult if we are not but we can learn. It was because your mother was sick from cancer and was not well enough in the last years of her short life and died when you were very young that you did not get all the love from your mother that you needed and then your father fell under that witchy stepmother who did not accept and love you and told your father that you were crazy because you could hear Nancy and the dolls talk to you that you did not get the love you needed from him that you have had so much trouble. Maybe because the stepmother was ignorant she did not know smart lonely children are creative and create friends like you did in their own minds. I wish you happiness and we will keep in touch. Your example of having your car repaired by a mechanic is true. The mechanic has learned to fix cars .I have spent many years learning how to fix broken minds. Maybe I can share some of my wisdom with you. Nancy was wise in getting yourself to me. I believe I have helped you. I believe you should talk with your other selves. You have a lot of intelligence and learning available to you and I also will be glad to be a resource to you. Don't worry about me having hurt feelings if you don't accept the offer, I won't have hurt feelings.

Sincerely, Dr. Young

Dr.young

The material you wrote has been read. I am going to hold it for a couple more days and reread it again. I fear it will not be too disturbing to dig up past history. Things are certainly a lot better than those good old days!

The attitude of all is better. I didn't realize I was so hard to get along with. The thing you said about being in hot water all the time, because I misinterpreted things. I've heard this from Keith recently. So maybe I do still take things wrong ,forgive me. And don't take it seriously if I say or act contrary. I know that most parts of myself are easy-going and think pretty straight. You remember that any untactful opinions are not the cause of alarm. Come to think of it, I have developed quite a knack of diplomacy. This no doubt, because I had to straighten out all feedings I had created by being too sensitive or guarded.

Our personal life is not all smooth. There is talk of separation from Keith and I am for it unless he can modify himself some. He is good in many respects. Offers security financially and emotionally if we can pay the price for it, but oh how hard. What a price! He is good for Roxanne, and Bernas is perhaps more at home with him, because she feels wiser than he and can give him patience. This is important for she can feel important to someone that way. He has said we must not be in a hurry about going,

59

but take some time and prepare ourselves better. I must get busy, because it is one o'clock. I haven't dressed yet, today has slipped away. . Sincerely, Bernice.

Bernice came for a visit. Actually it was Nancy. Nancy said: "well I got her back here again. Anne is still angry at you. She says, you called her a prostitute."

"Nancy, I know from what you have written, that you would like to have more time with me. I'm sorry there is so much to do and so little time. I am torn between giving you more time and working on the problems or causes of much trouble. You are not sick, and the proverb that the squeaking wheel gets the grease is what is happening here. I know that isn't fair, because you are doing so much to get the rest of yourself here, and the most I can do is give you credit for what you're doing in getting my help for them. I hope my recognition of all you are doing for the good of yourselves and my appreciation for your helpfulness will help some in supporting you in your efforts. Please keep up the good work. Now, I feel it's very important to do some work with Anne. I hope you can listen in while I talk to her. I would like to talk to Anne now. "

" Anne!, I would like to talk to you now. I've been thinking of you and about how we got into the difficulty we're having and how to straighten out a misunderstanding. When I talked about forgiveness, and Christ forgiving a woman for her transgressions, I do not know whether I used the word prostitute, or it was implied by you. I do not recall exactly what I said. Anyway, I did not think of you as being a prostitute, nor mean to accuse you of being one. I apologize for the mistake I made. I feel like I put my foot in my mouth, and you shoved it up to my knee. I don't mean by that to be critical of you but just explain how I feel. I notice that you are very sensitive to criticism and believe something in your past has sensitized you to cause strong reactions to criticism. I would like to check this out and see if we find some information about whether something happened in the past but is still affecting you in the present. I would like for you to let your mind, respond to this question. Have you at some time been scolded for something you did not do? If you have, please be with me now so I can talk with you about it."

Emotions of agitation and distress occurred. A child began to cry and say repeatedly: "I didn't do it."

I asked:"you didn't do what?"

"I did not hurt the baby.
"

"Tell me what happened."

"They went for a walk and left me to take care of the baby. The baby started crying for no reason, and I couldn't get her to stop. When they came back the baby was screaming and Mary Lou said: "you hurt the baby." I didn't do it. I didn't do nothing. I didn't do it!
"

"What did Mary Lou do with the baby?
"

"She gave her the bottle and the baby stopped crying."

"The baby was hungry, and that's why she was crying, and you didn't do anything to cause her to cry. Mary Lou was only 16 years old when this happened. She made a mistake and thought you had hurt the baby and did not understand that the baby was hungry. Her mother instinct told her to begin to nurse the baby and the baby stopped crying. Mary Lou scolded you for something you did not do. I am sorry that happened. I would like to undo that mistake. I understand you did not do anything to hurt the baby. You are a good girl, and you are not a bad girl. You were only seven or eight years old when this happened. They should not have given you this responsibility and blamed you for what happened. You were too young to understand and know what to do. At that time, you did not know to give the baby the bottle of milk and you may not have understood that the baby was hungry. Please let me take away the hurt you have had because you were so misunderstood and been scolded for something you did not do. When someone accuses us of something we did not do it hurts and it hurts if we are not believed when we say we did not do it . we need to be believed and we need an apology. You did the best that you could do and I am proud of you for taking care of the baby. I give you an apology for your sister's mistake. I hope you can feel better now. You are a good girl. You deserve praise and appreciation for all the help you gave your sister by taking care of the baby. You made it possible for Mary Lou and Herman to take an evening walk hand in hand , I believe you did love the baby and would not hurt her . I know it hurts to be so misunderstood, I hope you can feel believed and understood now and you will not feel hurt and angry now. I understand how you have felt this hurt all of this time and every time there is a misunderstanding and you are accused of something that is not true the hurt feelings come up again I hope this makes the hurt stop hurting now Thank you for telling me about it so I could help you which makes me feel better too because I like to help. You can go back to sleep feeling good and I will talk to Anne now. "

"Anne! I hope this little girl can feel much better now. I hope this helps you feel less sensitive to criticism now. I like the way you stand up for yourself and you are good for defending yourself. You need this from you to counter balance the submissiveness that has come from being so beaten down by criticism and abusive behaviors of others. I respect you for your spunk. Maybe this will take the 'chip off of your shoulder"

"I hope so. I know that getting angry at people who seem to be criticizing me is one of my problems. It is also bothering me that I tend to be scolding myself for this. This is like my sister. I get angry at myself for being like her".

Dear Dr. Young.
Things are really not going so well. We're all together now and it is very quiet and no one pushes anyone around or makes anyone do anything they don't want to do. So mostly, we don't do anything. There is a strange one that is too afraid to go anywhere and so we stay inside and she shakes and trembles until she is the only one left and the rest of us can't feel anything but we are not dead. Last Sunday she talked to me for a few words, but we have no terror with her. Once I tried to see if I could approach her and I felt with her. It was so odd. We were in pain and all her teeth were being extracted ,some whole and some in tiny fragments. I was so surprised when I came back for air to find there was not really blood all over my face. I had felt it and even smelled it. Sometimes we are fine for hours at a time, but we have to be careful or we start getting trouble. We can't bring her to you because she is too scared. I'm sorry we had to withdraw from school. At the next semester, we can go again, This was our last week at this college. So we wanted to finish it badly. I hope I can help this one the way you helped me. It's not too good to just sit in this room, Well, we do drive the children to school every morning and go to the market, and that's something. And no one feels angry at you now so that's better. Sincerely ,Ruth and all.

Bernice sent to me a card attached to a sheet of paper. On the card she wrote: "I'm sitting by the window with a pen in my hand and this card, and I am lying there on the bed and sitting over there laughing. Those are empty shells because I have evidence that I am sitting here by the window and writing this. I know three people can not wear the same clothes at the same time. I know I'm real. They are illusions."

On the paper, there are three entries dated with the month and day, but not the year.

It was less than a half hour ago that I retired, and I was reading. I must've been drifting off to sleep. I seemed to hear a voice calling me by name and telling me to listen. I don't know if I was asleep or not, If it was a dream or really happened, but I was aware of being pushed out completely, I felt as if my head would literally burst or pop. Suddenly, before I was gone, I was wide awake and myself. I don't mind saying I felt frightened somewhat, but not so much as I used to be. In some respects it is a little as if I was being hypnotized, and going, yet I know that I was the only one in the room. I would jump right up anyway and stay awake for most of the night. So I have decided to write down an account of it each time. And maybe I will be able to understand it. I know by now that it's a harmless experience, but disturbing nevertheless.

It just happened again, all suddenly there was a dizzy, whirling sensation, seemed as if I was rapidly (very rapidly), sinking, So fast, in fact, that I couldn't keep up with myself. Quite suddenly, I seemed to be standing across the room, leaning on the chest, laughing. I seemed to rise to a sitting position and still I was lying on the bed. I seemed to be saying: " See, you can't get up, you just can't make it." Someway, it seemed like a laughing matter, and yet, it was very distressing. It must've been probably seconds, although it seemed like a very long time. I snapped awake, and as usual, my pulse was hammering like mad."

It almost happened again, but not quite. The dizzy spiraling has started, and something, I'm not sure what, was looking,. I thought, well here we go again and this time I'm going to find out what goes on, only I snapped awake immediately. Now these are not hallucinations. I've had them before, or are they?"

I , Dr, Young, replied: "It is true that these are illusions. Two of you are not writing, that is. They are two of your alters who are able to visualize themselves to you. You can learn to communicate with them by talking to them because they are real parts of your mind. Being able to visualize them will help in your communication. For example, you saw that one of them was laughing, and the other was distressed because of inability to get up. It is a hypnotic state. If you are not frightened about it, you may be able to remain in that state and communicate with yourself. Others have been able to communicate in their sleep and solve problems. You may be able to do this too, if you learn to use this ability. Your awakening when frightened is an example of your unconscious protecting you as I told you it would when I explained that your unconscious would protect you when I use hypnosis by awakening you if it senses some danger. I hope your unconscious that guards you will get this message that what is happening is not dangerous and will not awaken you in fright and will let you use this communication constructively when the' mothering one' comes to comfort you and holds your hand, and you understand that the hand is cold, because your mother and your good friend who died who seem to have been incorporated in this helping alter, would have a cold hand. That is no reason to fear because they are still much alive within your mind. You do not have to be frightened by the cold hand, because you can understand now that their spirit is still with you. This is an example of the rich resources your unconscious mind can provide for you. There is much love and wisdom within yourself. This is not a psychotic symptom and I will not say you are crazy. I am glad that you trust me enough now to tell me what you experience. One patient was able to assemble all of the selves in a conference during her sleep and solve some problems in relationships and use the wisdom of the unconscious mind to help solve some problems, all while she was still getting some sleep. You have an unusual gift, and I hope you can use it.

Bernice must have brought this information in by hand because it is not folded for an envelope. It was not dated and I do not know when it was brought in.

"It's annoying, this pulling in many directions. The outer world, the housework, a dining room set that needs refinished , redone ,or thrown out and we- bought, the curtains last May, and still not hung on the service porch, which reminds me. There is probably a new basket of clothes to wash today and a box of apples from Bonny Doone I'm supposed to can are something, and the yard that wants to have a fishpond and some new soil and flower beds and a hundred new plants to line the 900 foot driveway and a whole new set of ideas cry out every time I step outside. I could create a whole park here. Meantime, the walnut trees are casting their nuts and want to be picked up and the leaves need raking and school offers a test tonight and a long assignment Friday. And I think it would be nice to lay on the grass and pet Conda, the dog, on the head and watch the sky – except that I really would rather be writing. And inside the head the little schisms move relentlessly – the little children that inhabit me – I feel fuzzy little creases that separate the mind, they clamor for air. It's time that winter is coming soon and one shouldn't stay under a cold muddy porch, nor should they stay lost in the woods or hover in a corner afraid to talk. Nor should I be slowed down, while the gears grind and mesh and nothing but dreams come forth. Speaking of dreams, I dreamed a funny sort of dream. It was a wedding of the little blue-eyed blonde haired girl who comes to me in dreams from time to time (in color yet) and she was getting married in a Swedish folk dance sort of ceremony. I saw this little girl's mother and she was me when I'm at my worst, when I 'm like meanness. Her back was up and determined and somewhat angry too – but she took all the credit for the silliest ceremony ,– the folk dancing couple that said: "Now hear us all , The time has come for this man to take a wife and etc.". Finally the little blue eyed girl finished her service, and she came to me and hugged me and looked up with her tears swimming in her eyes and I knew I'd taken care of this little girl long a go. And I said, "You will always be happy" and I felt sort of silly, because her mother, that was me, also stood there looking on with disapproval, and I thought " oh heck, I don't like her much anyway"(the mother that is), but enough of that dream.

The question is, how do I get my population together , my children from woods and porch and city street and set them together and teach them that I'm the mother in this family? (How come I never get to quit raising kids?).

It would be easier if they were all separate entities. Then I could say you do this assignment, and you do that. Instead I have to say take turns. You do this, and you do that and if number one wants to build a fishpond maybe number two will kindly do my homework – but really, someone must write – never demean this intention – someone intends to write and never will there be peace until I do – and you may not believe I can do it, but on my honor I must and I will so help me God! So help me God.

I will tell the world, whether they listen or not, that they have to love their neighbors – that no one is so far gone that persistent love can't reach them. There's not enough love in this world and people just have to help create it. And I'll tell the world that the older generation is not useless and done with and the young must be corporative with them. They will have their day. But they can have the whole world, especially while blaming the world. For every injustice within it, like it or not, they are a part of it now. They are here and can be heard. But they didn't find all the answers in 20 years. They are only as bold as they are because of the parents who help them by

being more permissive. Instead of blaming their parents – give them credit for having created such open-minded and brilliant products. As themselves, they didn't come out of a cabbage leaf. They were born and nurtured and loved and given to by parents who had other parents. And if they say, we have the courage to change the world, they could add because our parents taught us to think for ourselves to make and learn from mistakes and we will build on this to spread the good news of individuality. But don't forget the rootstock. Don't call them unknowing and unlearned and a generation removed.

It is a brave New World, all right, but needs tempered by love.

Anyway – I have got to do something soon or I'll burst my seams !

Add a dozen me's

Do you believe I can? Write, I mean. I can."

This was not signed but looks like it was written by B. W., which is the code for Bernice, the writer. I did not answer it. She has a rather simple, parental, but sincere message, and one may see why Anne says she is stupid.

"I found an article in a Good Housekeeping magazine that interests me. As always, I am on the lookout for information that I can apply to my own unhappy mental condition. How I wish I could talk it over with Dr. Young… Yet he probably would not give any serious consideration to it as it would disrupt his theory of the multiple personalities. This article totally characterizes my grief to a T. It describes what I have been through over and over again. In fact, I am just recovering from several days in a very depressed and unhappy state of mind. I have always bitterly maintained that I was not a masochist……. I do not want to suffer, but grief, as explained by this psychiatrist is a normal thing. For many years I have staunchly insisted that I have never felt grief for my mother, dead 26 years. Not me, tough good old practical me… If someone is dead, well they are dead, and all the remorse in the world cannot replace them… Anyway, I told myself that I was perfectly capable of taking care of myself… I didn't ever need a mother… Not even as an independent little child, did I cry for my mother… At least I didn't think I did… Maybe a lot of tears have been shed after all in disguise. Now the connection, I have made this my flimsy structure which began to fall apart five years ago when the best friend I have had in my whole life contracted, or more correctly discovered, that she had cancer in a very acute stage of development (my mother died of cancer). This person, (the name has been cut out), had been like a mother to me for 2 ½ years. If one could choose a mother, I'm sure my choice would have been her. Yet, when she, a very robust appearing person, was found to be dying of cancer in the thyroid gland, too far advanced for emergency ,surgery, I too developed the same symptoms within my thyroid gland. So positive were the indication cancer that immediate surgery was done and the tumor was removed and found to be benign. This was a product, no doubt an attempt to die along with my friend. After the death I began to "go to pieces ". The symptoms listed in this article might be my own description of myself in a cycle of torture. Now maybe it is a set of subconscious related grief for my mother reawakened by the circumstances just described. If so, I hope I can understand and work through it and end this private hell. I can not possibly say if this is true, but if so, why don't I separate the mental process into categories? Why not regress through hypnosis and bring these things to the surface? I have so long insisted that my mother was nothing to me... not even a memory... Yet that is part of a human attitude. Maybe I suppressed grief for her as a child.. I don't know. I do know that since"(deleted)" death I have had dreams in which she comes to me, it seems to be (deleted), yet she says she is my mother. It happened last night. I had a difficult night with tormenting nightmares all night and then someone came down the hall. I heard the footsteps so plainly. I thought it was Mike, my husband, and whoever it was sat on the side of the bed and began talking, as always, "now don't cry like this. I expect better things of you than this." It took my hand. The hand was so cold that I knew it was not alive. I jumped up and began to scream. It is funny, I never really see a face, just a form. Sometimes it just stands above my bed, or in the doorway, and I know it is there. It isn't like a hallucination, I have had those and they are different, this is more like... I know I can't really view it is a spirit, but(incomplete)."

Unfortunately, this was never brought up in an individual session and is unfinished business. I would not have told her this was self-pity. Such grief should be accepted and resolved as a normal human response

I have seen a home movie made before my friend died in which Iwas well and happy The children were dressed in beautiful clothes I had made and were happy. I think I know now why I fell apart.

.

.

This note had a handwritten note at the top. "Everything looked dark, don't be offended, you did more than I give you credit for here"

" I'm in a "blue" mood, as I have been for four days. I'm discouraged and pessimistic about the future, wondering what is the wise thing for me to do. I don't really feel like going back to Dr. Young again After two years, I am still the same unhappy, moody person that I was. When all is said and done very little has been accomplished. He has been on his tour of my mind... He has worked hard at achieving what he wanted to achieve, the separation of me. Well, perhaps that is unfair... The separation was there to begin with. He just pleases himself by exploring it at my expense and in the face of my pleading for him to pay attention to the visible problems that I've faced. I do not blame him actually... I might do this same thing under the same circumstances, but no doubt he feels that he has done the right thing. Some things are definitely improved. I haven't so many fears, I am able to go to sleep or walk around a darkened room without being seized with panic, I very seldom hear "footsteps " at night and it has been a long time since the doors opened at night and closed silently while a cold wind blew into the room without a left evidence. My night visitors have-not sat on my bed and touched me with cold hands. For months, though, as I look back I realized they only came when I was deeply depressed and suicidal and that they always comforted me. I had no need to fear them as I did. I have new viewpoints on some things. For instance, I no longer allow myself to be" used". I am less inclined to self depreciation. I seldom have as severe headaches, I don't always become sick at my stomach when I am in a crowd. Yet I am still a very unhappy person most of the time. I am not in favor of any more emphasis be placed on "how many" personalities I am. Instead, I want some discussion to pertain to me as a "total person". I have enough communication with and knowledge about myself and I know I can intelligently face what I must about myself. What prevents me from being a happy, productive and worthwhile individual? I think, on the one hand, that I should go back for the next appointment and explain to him and see if he is willing to deal with me as a single unit. If he won't, then I wouldn't have to go up back again. Still, if I have as much difficulty talking to him as I have in times past, I will only place myself in the predicament of having to listen to the same stories that he sold me a dozen times before like lack of appreciation, etc. on my part. I am not convinced that I can refrain from anger. If I don't feel at least that he is looking at both sides of my story and not just "assuming" that I am to blame for all my marriage difficulties, I won't go back.. I want to work with him, because I started with him, also because I do like him as a person. But that doesn't make me a well person either. I just don't have confidence enough in myself to deal with the present problem to face him without feeling that he is going to criticize and censor and ridicule me

(there is half a page of blank paper and then this note on the following page the writing seems to have a different attitude).

"I fussed about trivial things for a while too. I am missing out on youth, etc.. Now I can say with all sincerity and truthfulness, I am perfectly content with myself.. I don't mind being thirty one years old, and I don't even mind being overweight. I might lose it if I found some way, in the meantime, I am not perturbed about it. Anne wants to have some time now. So bye.(This probably was Nancy).

Anne is getting sleepy. And she is a good girl too... Now I am . I was a real trial, though... But I was so mad and so bitter, and I wanted to fight everything and everybody. Well all my hate has been reasoned away and all my fury has been spent. I still don't stand for any crap from people and I won't. I feel very glad that I have been so forgiven... I shouldn't have been so high-handed. Well the past is done. I am for progress. I am satisfied with everything now. Am too tired to say much more so, all from me.BA.

This is some undated poetry:
" I know I have something to say.
When the wind calls out.
And the curtains sway.
I know this call from the ancient past
I must have my say.
And say it fast.
I'm not really long for this world.
I know it's true.
When I'm free, unfurled.
So I hurried and scurried for paper and pen.
To store my thoughts.
Ere they reach the wind.
Oh yes I know – I know and am glad.
No one can force me or hold or scold.
For I am free now.
From the other soul.
I love to live.
To think-to give."
Below this in large and scrawling script is the following writing: "God what's the matter with this fool.'

My Lord, first have a blasted poet, and then we'd have a thinker, which is worse, and a lost soul, who wants a body – and an old battered one that cries for Papa and a Savior of all and then we get an active one, who gives them all "The divil." Then by golly, somebody had a baby in all this mess. We have a baby and then ,oh brother, let me tell you, this is one old villain who's just getting fed up_ Burp the baby people"

Nancy takes care of the baby..

Ha ha ha ha."

The above is obviously Anne. It expresses both her disdain and humor.

"This has been one day of confusion. I think I'm missing out on a good deal of life. I know, I am one person-I think, so I have to be! All people have mood swings, but that doesn't change the basic fact that they are one. What is a thought in my mind that influences me to say all these bad things and also to get all mixed up and actually think I am a part writing things and sign them by initials? The most disturbing thing to me, however, is the way I keep hearing, or more correctly, feeling the impression of thoughts so strongly impressed on my mind that they seem like voices. They can't be voices. Phrases like," I hate you", " I hate everything , I wish I were dead,-get a rope and hang yourself, cut off your head with an electric saw." It's maddening-believe me. I have a hard time thinking in terms of sanity. If the doctor wonders why I keep thinking I'm crazy, he should be tuned in on my line sometimes. Just last week, I was on my way to Foothill Farms, stopped at the store to cash a check, had my driver's license out for identification and when I started put it away the voice said, "don't bother putting it away, You will need the driver's license because you will have to show it to the Highway Patrol when you have a wreck in a few minutes". I felt shaken up, and I was unsure until I got home safely after this happened. It's like someone is telling me to destroy myself, such as impressions that I should drive in front of a big truck or a train or to drive off a bridge into the water. Is there some part of me that wants death so badly it would destroy all of me? For a while , I felt suicidal, but now I don't. I feel that I must live if for nothing else than for the children. But I want to live for myself also, now that I don't feel suicidal any more, a thought comes so strongly demanding that I take my life. Is this just negative thoughts that everyone has ? My head aches and my neck hurts. Bernice.

This is Sun 10 p.m. Dr. Young, This is us again with all our ups and downs. One hour a week doesn't give time enough for all that needs to be said. So since you have repeatedly said to correspond, I am taking advantage once again of the postal department, or maybe I'll drop by in person tomorrow."

(BE is the code I gave for Bernice's 'evaluator', called " Eva"),

"Dr young. For identity purposes, I am BE. I have more to say than I can possibly communicate at this time… However, a few issues are at hand, and I would like to give you my viewpoint. An issue began with a proposal that has been made to change therapists. There are so many ways to consider this and I fail to see that the final result would be any real advantage. Especially since the change will involve a certain adjustment, once again our working methods. Also, where in this city, could we find a doctor who would be able to understand as much as you do, or just plain " tolerate" as much as you do and still be optimistic enough to offer hope? The personal, or" extra," interest you have shown has been rejected as not necessarily helpful by some… At the same time it has been absolutely invaluable to others. This would not be forthcoming from another doctor, I am sure, and I am hesitant to change for the simple reason that there are few who could understand the different sides as you do, and yet, a consultation might be helpful to BB (Bernice) and the other personalities who need confirmation of your conclusions, I wonder if, after all that has gone on, would it really make a difference? If she doesn't believe you, along with all the accumulation of evidence in the form of writing etc. then would it make a difference if an angel from heaven told her it was true? There are several separate personalities, very definitely, and BB seems to be the only one who disputes this. I think this is because she seems to have an awareness of all that goes on. Much has happened lately, much has been written. I have just finished a couple of hours reading. I see no reason why so much fuss and denials should be made. What is more reasonable or logical than the fact that the human mind consists of components? I'm doing some research on personalities… Normal and abnormal and the development of personalities came up for my interest, and human nature, and I will see if I can find any answers to the" how come" to this personal situation. Along with what I can find in publications (this is not in a request for information from you), as with the hypnosis, as I am going to take a long time on this in connection with school and I will find material faster than I can read and make notes in my spare time. I'm encouraging as much note taking for ourselves as possible, and I thought this might be something that would help "us" communicate and perhaps might help us unify the" total person". I am going to keep an accurate record of the changes as they occur. I have thought it might be helpful if we could find if there are any certain patterns that are followed. So far, there seems to be no indication of this.

There is just not enough self communication to talk this out with folks in myself. I mean to see if there is a disturbing element in the form of another part or as this has been suggested it comes from the lack of knowing how to work together. But no… From somewhere comes this destructive thing as BB wrote recently that, one time, she was suicidal and now, when she doesn't consider suicide, from somewhere comes the strong impression (voice?) she should go ahead and die" or the impression, almost in command, form from somewhere that she should run in front of a train off a bridge into the river or something equally fatal This to me is foreign thought . I really hope that no one of me will act on such suggestions or be out of reality enough to respond to these urges. I hesitate to believe that "A." is this disturbing. While she is a little on the active side, I think all in all she is a very needed addition, She has suggested in her notes that you explore the" segment' of each individual's unconscious to see if any one of us is bringing the torture unconsciously. She admittedly does not like BF and she laughs at a lot things, but so do I. I feel that there is need for a more constant working on this problem. From one visit to the next so many changes have occurred and it is impossible for you to talk with any one very often. For a while, Mike was a help. But he is a person with a short span of interest. For this reason, I wonder if we would benefit more if you saw him some time instead of us. And you can help him to promote communication and understanding needed. I would love to do it myself, but it isn't possible to be upfront very often. Also there is a whole society of us inside, but there is the usual need for a tangible person outside. Too bad while Mike isn't stable enough without encouragement himself. I'm fascinated with the idea that inside of his psyche there might be some "lost" part that would equal motivation… It is his biggest lack. He has lots of ideas, but they just fade out with the time it takes to think them. This is very frustrating to some of us. Is it the backwardness of our own backwardness in the form of Bernas and the independence of B B which has about the same value as just holding back and being afraid. I know I get over enthusiastic, but how I wish I could have time enough to express all my thoughts and ideas and conclusions. I guess that is the big trouble with this life, which ever of us gets a little time out always has so much to say that we fail to give much thought to them on the inside. Well I think of them, but I am guilty of not giving the call to the other people inside. Maybe we get enough of one another on the inside. One thought I did have was this. Is it possible that the child, being alone for the most part, and with little help, except self-help, incurs the components of the mind to develop as individuals instead of integrating as the natural tendency seems to be? So that as a child the self communication was the answer to the need for other people, yet now, as an adult it isn't possible to be satisfied with just a self and the world and because the development was separate in the whole or total person cannot get together well enough to relate properly to the world around us? Of course, how it happened is not so important as how to get together again. There has to be an answer, and I am going to find it if at all possible. When there is a crisis, immediate access to outside help is almost necessary. You of course, can not fill this and neither can I. For example when a certain one, I'm not sure who, gets upset reasoning from the inside is vain for she grabs her head and shakes thoughts away and fails to get or recognizes no good from internal attempts at reasoning. I, and others leave messages on paper, and she hasn't learned to look for help in them at the time of distress, instead ,becoming offended in the attempt to help and the situation is made worse by the misunderstanding between the two of them. How much the better for both of them to work together to try to solve the conflict. Another thing, I believe, is unbalanced, is the work load... I sometimes I think that Bernas gets an unfair share of the work, and she does stick with it where as some of us are always going somewhere or grabbing a book or heading for the typewriter... Like me tonight... I could be ironing, but I did feel like I should send some communication to you and Bernas works very well and very efficiently. Frankly, things are discouraging sometimes for all . Bernas is the one who always is so angry and is going to "go away and never come back". Well, of course, no one is going anywhere, but she gets so furious and acts like she is going to go into orbit in a minute. Only she loses the steam spluttering around..

Oh darn, goodnight or good morning. It's almost 2 in the morning BE

(This letter came to me with some very good news. This is an example that the unconscious mind can produce resources that are hard to believe.)

"It is a good thing to be a whole person, it is better still to be an at home person. Who knows one's self as well as I know me. I am sure that of all the people in the world, I am one of the most fortunate, how good to live!

I have two more weeks to wait before I see the Dr. Young again. I am looking forward to seeing him, but I don't feel the desperation that I once did, because I am doing so well that I can't "need" him now. I must go in again and let him try to contact the infant part… If he wants to… It causes no trouble, but I think it should be in touch with the rest of us. I also must go back and let him see how I am a person now…. I will do anything he asks now without fear, without any fear at all. If he wants to speak to us individually that will be fine… "(I am so agreeable that I am just wonderful!).

Tonight I was thinking of the bitterness, the suspicion, distrust, and doubt that we used to know. How good it is to be free from all that… I can't be involved in that ever again, because I understand too much now. Anne was held down so long that she became unpleasant and did cause some distress… Bernas was too weary to want to live and thought she would be better off if she were going to God… Anne is free now and she isn't angry anymore. I am so glad that I can sit here and write…BE is so glad she can think. We are all so happy.

Think of all the things that lie ahead of us… Think of the good life ahead… We live, we really live! I think! I think that I will never get over the wonder of being a person. Free. Not a part, not a ghostly specter wandering through the darkness… Not a nocturnal zombie rising from my bed and digging in the back of the closet for my old faded Chinese robe that was so loose and comfortable… God, I was barely alive… I used to sit by the living room window at night with any old scrap of paper that I could find and scribble my thoughts in the dimness of the streetlights coming through the window… It hardly occurred to me as a possibility that I was enough actually to live… I used to look at the sleeping children and wonder what I would do with them, if I was confronted with the task of caring for them. Poor Bernice… No wonder she was complaining about a life… No wonder she was so mixed up inward and out! No, it is not a good thing to be separated. I want to know more and more about me. We are so proud… We couldn't breathe properly, and we couldn't think correctly… We were lost in a mad scramble, and we each lived so briefly and so uncoordinated that we couldn't mingle with people… But we are very much a person now.

(note_The" pesonality" writing this assumed the name of Captain and the initials of BC without any input from me)

Think about me right forever now. This is the first day of September, and I "lived" for the first time the 18th of October 1959. I am so pleased with the last year. I remember so well the day I was "born". It was around the afternoon, I suddenly began to have an awareness. I hurt inside with the feeling of expanding emptiness, and I could hardly see. I perceived outlines and shapes, and everything appeared hazy. I think it must have taken an hour or more for me to have complete clearness, and little by little, I realized what was going on then. I "knew" that I was in concert with others and myself. They knew of my presence and somehow relayed the message to me that they were in distress. I found the most natural thing in the world for me was to help them. I knew that I had a great helper in Dr. Young, and I felt calmly sure that he would be very glad to know me. Inside the house, things were unreal... It wasn't until I walked outside and sat on the brick fence and looked at the flowers growing in little pots and in narrow fenced off beds that I felt I knew the world. Especially do I remember some red petunias. They were in the tiniest little place and completely surrounded with cement, yet they had at least half a hundred blooms. They were isolated...But they were doing just fine. I knew that I would do just fine also... And I have. We all have. Captain.

Nancy: I think I've had things so much easier than so bad. I love life, and I have always found a great deal to live for where ever or whenever, I have had awareness. I have done my part of troublemaking too... But I think I have likewise corrected myself quickly and easily. I am completely in love with life; I can make enough happiness now without feelng that I must be in touch with my doctor. Of course he is my friend and will always be my very favorite friend... I hope I never lose contact with him. And I won't... At least not in my mind where there are memories, and furthermore I don't think he will ever forget us either. I'm looking forward with eagerness to our move... Not all have reconciled and accepted the coming change of locale. I have obtained information from the college there and I believe we will enjoy this small-scale group. It was nice today to register for the coming semester there... So pleasant to see familiar faces and surroundings. I have four classes, this time, philosophy (for B E especially) psych again for all of us, speech and history of early civilization. I've tried again to get English X, I need the grammar badly, but she just shook her head and smiled, said:" no-no. It's unthinkable!"(. That's just what she thinks)."Nancy.

When the Captain came in, I welcomed her and said: "I'm so delighted that you are here. You indicate that you are in contact with all of the personalities. Is that correct?

"Yes, I seem to know all of them"

"Maybe you are the one I've been waiting for . I thought at one time that the one who said she had been a bad mother and she hid her children in fear, might know everyone and be a resource for bringing them together, but she said she was too frightened to do that. I believe that is to be your function. I tend to look for what seems to be a function or specialty, in a "personality" I am hopeful that you may be able to help with bringing all together. I want to give you my ideas about how to get yourself together. When I talked to your selves about the idea of integration,, they have become frightened because they think that that means they would no longer exist as if they were gotten rid of. I think the metaphor that Carl Jung , a psychiatrist, told about one of his patient's dream is a very helpful example of integration. She dreamed that she was in a place that felt very spiritual and like a temple. She was surrounded by tall pillars in a circle and the pillars began to fall inward over her and she was frightened that she would be destroyed. But the pillars came together over her head and joined together. She felt safe and completed. It was as if her mind had come together and from the center where she was, she felt she could coordinate all herself. Carl Jung said that an object that occurs frequently in art called a mandala, which is a quadrated circle which he believes is a representation of an integrated mind and in Hinduism and Buddhism it symbolizes wholeness . It looks like a wheel with spokes that are connected by the hub, which is the center of the self connected to the whole at the rim. The idea is that all the self is still there and is connected by the central Self. It is my hope that you can be the Self in the center and unite all yourself together. Each part of your mind has functions, values, needs , perspectives and potential solutions, which can be considered in making decisions for actions to be taken. I visualize the integrated personality as being a democracy in which you'll be,if elected ,president or commander in chief or captain and all the identities will be your constituents, and all will have a say in self-government, all the selves may or may not accept you as a commander-in-chief or captain unless you are best qualified to fulfill this function or role and they are assured of equal representation. There will be existence, liberty and justice for all. I will be glad to be your consultant if you so choose. There is still someone in your unconscious who is very miserable and wants to die. When the time seems right, she needs to be brought out and understood and helped. I am sure that she can be helped to live happily and also needs to accept that the others can live happily with her too. That will be a very important accomplishment. I look forward to working with you if you wish. See if everyone will sit around you in a circle, and you can begin to discuss how you'll work together. I believe it will take a great deal of patience, but you have that too. Bon voyage, Captain!

Nancy kept her promise to take Roxanne back to her old home. Fortunately, Roxanne was sufficiently settled into her new home, which made it easier for her to accept what they found. Nancy describes what she observed.

"Where the cabin stood, the trees now grow. The clearing that was our yard and field is only wooded timber land. The descendants of our beloved birds, our Cardinals and Whippoorwills, fly freely among the trees without the sights of people moving about in their midst. The blue birds have gone. They needed the clearing, the hedge rows which no longer support the mass of dew berry vines that hung so flush with dew berries large and moist which they ate. The fields where cotton grew or yams and corn and cane are covered with tall trees and under growth. The stumps that hung the plow and interrupted the rows of crops are decayed now and in their places stand arms of greenery. Will the well, that might be there still , though filled with debris in the rock walled circular depth that produced the clear cool water, ever fill the space again? There, under the cover of the decomposed leaves, must lie evidence of our cabin. There must be bits of melted glass from the Windows and fragments of cracked pottery and somewhere there is a small china doll buried with broken head. It would not be decomposed or burned.

The rains must fall from the heavens just the same, snow and frost in winter surely cover the branches, but no longer leaves the swirling patterns upon the window pane. Our cabin was beautiful. It was made of boards and nails and glass and moss grew on the roof where we laid the Apple rings and peach halves to dry in the sun . Over the new room, our father placed the shingles he made himself from splitting wood with a fro. His arms were strong. As he smoothed the boards, his veins on his hands stood out. He used a drawing knife to smooth the boards from which he made our swings.. He used a knife to split the wood into pliable strips from which he made baskets that we filled with eggs and bigger baskets taller than a child's head ,which the pickers used in the cotton fields. His big fingers wove a small basket too, very small, and painted green and this was given to a small child.

Our cabin was secure. Inside a fire blazed on the hearth. The winds might blow fiercely and angrily outside but our door was barred tight.

Around the fire we gathered and popped the corn we had grown and roasted the chestnuts we had gathered. The chestnut trees are gone from our mountain too, I am told. My heart felt barren, as I heard in a classroom 2000 miles away a quarter century later, that there were no more chestnut trees, because a blight had killed them all.

It rained softly on our cabin roof, softer than ever rains fall on any other place and the rain was not a thing to fear. There were gentle rains when we would threw our clothes off and ran over the soft ground and felt the drink that fed the thirsty soil. When lightening came and thunder sounded loud and sharp our cabin gave us courage. We pulled the covers close and snuggled in our fathers arms, and soon the storm would pass. Sometimes a rainbow arched across the sky and when it did, we'd follow it into the fields where it seemed to end ,there was a pot of gold buried there. We knew, our father said so. The rainbow moved so swiftly from us, taking with it the colored arch and the pot of gold, but never mind, it would come back again next time. And next time we would catch it sure.

Where our cabin stood, the trees grew large and the foliage was large and green. We plucked those leaves and folded them into cups fastened by a twig. We filled these with berries growing wild. We picked the leaves by the armful fastening them with tiny sticks, we made them into garments for play ,a cumberbund of soft leaves and from it hanging many strips of leaves attached one to another. We made crowns of leaves and garlands of clover, and we were royal subjects in this land of ours where once our cabin stood, and now it is overgrown and no one would ever know that once a home was there .

Nearby, a rock loomed large where we had played. If I could camp again on that, my vast estate, I'd go.

Were cabin stood a vast sorrow came. An angel passed darker than the night and took the spirit it came for. The flowers bloomed in spring as usual, but no one loved them. Insects sang their evening song, but no voices blended with them anymore.

To our cabin, another came, not to revive a lifeless home but to scatter the carcass. The dust was wiped from the window panes but none could see from them as they were draped heavily and none could touch. The fire was bright, but a screen was kept in front of it, which kept us from the closeness of roasted chestnuts. The inhabitants left one by one, and soon there remained nothing but the friendly rock in the woods and the talking trees and the cautious rabbits. The enemy would not stop. Each day the threat grew worse and we knew we had to leave our beloved cabin and we did but our spirit was left hidden safely under the big rock and none would wait for us to bring a doll along.

We traveled for years without a soul. For now, and a quarter century, away in another land, we know we must have our home again. So we returned and the cabin is gone. The mountain has come down to swallow our cabin and the woods keep secret the cabin site. But I know it is there, and I will go to the woods and find the markers that remain. I'll clear that land and build a cabin once again. I'll find the evil spirit, and I'll devour it. I'll hold it and the sun can shine again and the rain will be gentle and the tender flowers will replace the burrs and all will know and never more forget this place were once our cabin stood.

Dear Nancy and all ,

I am very sorry that your cabin is no longer there. I can understand your feeling a great loss. T he home means a lot more to a child, than adults realize. One child mourning the loss of her home said of the new home "this house does not know me." It's like being uprooted to be moved about. You lost your mother, your father and your home. It is appropriate for you to feel much grief. I understand your wish to rebuild the cabin, but it may be wisest to tell it goodbye and feel the grief and establish a new home. All of you have survived and are getting back together. You are overcoming the terrible effects of your losses. Do not give up. With compassion, Dr. Young.

Dr. Young

From where I stand and now.. In a state of question, I wish to go on to something more definite, more concrete. By way of a brief review, which I realize is not necessary except to clarify what I wish to do. I go back to the state of confusion and perplexity in which I first approached you. I had lived for most of my life in a somewhat limited sort of way... Barren and inadequate-not a feeling of inadequacy, rather a lack of something. I just plain wasn't all there! I had a deep feeling about this; it isn't easy to know that something is missing, especially when remarks etc. from others make it evident that they know it also. This was not all oversensitivity attitude, though no doubt much of it was It is humiliating to be an inferior individual... Especially when you know, deep inside that you have that "missing something"... If you could just get hold of it! We know it is there, but cannot express it or it struggles inside, and always arrives just a little too late to be an effective response. You just somehow don't jive too well with other people and, by nature, this leaves a hurt and emptiness in life that results in all kinds of defense reactions. I was never satisfied with my relationships with other people, because with people who either had less to organize than I or who had managed to organize a certain portion of their capabilities in any way that pleased and satisfied them were either, after a brief acquaintance, boring and dull and without depth or on the other hand, there were those who were able to manifest more in the way of intelligence found me to be the dull one which actually left me in a sort of no man's land. The potentialities dormant in my make-up make me restless , a sort of misfit… An odd one to all appearances. But the only trouble was. I KNEW that somehow I was as good if not better than the mass of humanity. Conflict, and inner battles, neurosis, but in spite of all the pessimism that I felt at times there was an optimistic gleam, for the most part, I can't keep this to myself. But I did know that I was going to make the grade some day.

Then as you began contacting the "parts," or whatever term is best to use, something began to happen! With each new one added there was a change. It was a very strange thing to live with. Now I am me, and now I am not, but still I am! I don't understand many things, for one thing, It almost seems that they had to be given permission to be. To deny them , once I was aware of them, brought all kinds of different reactions that is, actually, a story in itself

I wouldn't take seriously for one minute some of the things that happened to me if they were told me by someone else, yet all was still not well entirely. Actually from you, I learned of (N) (A) (W) (F)."

(F is code for Bernas who said"I was first").

"I believe I am correct in stating that both E and C came independently of therapy. Something I am sure is still missing. With the addition of each of these new parts there was a period of adjustment. That was remarkably similar in each case. Excepting (BC), (captain)which was a very peaceful, almost spiritual experience, every " part" went through a cycle of growth before settling down. At first the impression was one of "well here I am… Now everybody sit up and take notice! I HAVE ARIVED, there was always a degree of aggression, some more than others, but all were somewhat on the defensive. Perhaps they could be likened to a newly released convict who appears as an ingrate in so many cases, puzzling people who wonder at his hostility and lack of gratitude. It was as if an almost orderly sequence of development took place, maybe it was part of a trial and error, but it wasn't unlike stages of a child progresses through on a much more rapid scale, of course. Without exception, each addition has been a thing in my favor, by agreeing, by accepting them I can have a peaceful life; denial or even doubt and skepticism or decision to ignore them as entities is a sure way to become very distressed and open the door to confusion again. There are other forces at work, which I am aware of but not in alignment with. Usually, if I avoid fatigue or minor physical illnesses, I can reason with and control them… Sometimes they have the upper hand. I am not asking to deal in a therapeutic manner with these because I do not altogether approve of your therapy and because I do believe that if I can know these forces then I can work out a happy solution. I think it impossible in the final analysis for a third (or second) person to actually adjust another life, advice and encourage yes, but the final results are, I believe, the most personal thing a person can or will ever do in life.

Now to come up to date, there are no doubts in my mind that the personalities exist… I know them well, some better than others. I cannot switch at will, nor can I always get a communication from a specific one. But I find this is not necessary, though I think it would be an advantage to be able to do so in some instances, at least. I know that they are here, but where they began I am not sure.

I try to explain it as a strictly therapeutic thing, on a hypnosis basis. Surely it is not impossible, if a mind would accept the suggestion that a harmless postage stamp is a strong mustard plaster and will blister the skin of the person conditioned to believe it then by suggestion, one could no doubt be led to a state of separation of psyche. Yet it would seem that these would dissolve after awhile, and not hold life and recognition as dearly as some of these do, protesting about being referred to as a " part" or considered less than a whole personality, complete with its own set of reasoning power, and in many cases making more sense than the original.

As for as a transference basis that someone suggested, I personally reject this, for , while I could not prove on a scientific viewpoint, I know personally that I have kept my logic and emotion separate. And I believe you will agree that my emotions have been detached and much more negative than positive in nature arguing every hour of the way. It would hardly seem likely that I tried to please you!

I don't know how a control could be worked out to make a true scientific research project, one case proves little anyway… And to a certain extent. I'm not a good subject as I have had too much work done already and know too many of your views, yet I believe that I am as objective as anyone. I really am not trying to prove anything. I just want to see and understand. I do believe that it is within the realm of man to know what he consists of. And I think the avenue to peace on Earth is through self understanding. I see no reason why we have to forever accept the explanation that we are not supposed to know everything. I feel very deeply that much good, could be accomplished by more concern with what goes on inside man's own mind and less concerned with space control (unless the space is inside). I hope we can come to a mutual agreement on this. The main points that I ask to be observed is that we be perfectly honest –I shall accept what is found. You will phrase your questions in a manner that is not biased to bring the answer you wish. After all if we are looking for truth we have to accept what is really there without building a structure. I wish to add that for what my opinion is worth the separation of personality purposely is probably a very good way to get a reluctant patient to look at himself. Also I ask that you not use accusations when dealing with my parts. I am beginning to like me and I disagree with you all together on the theory you use such as A is mistreating F. It should not be a bone of contention between us. However, since I(BE) am determined to be very open-minded, and if evidence indicates such is the case, then you are right and I will deal with my offending part. There is a destructive force, I know, that is true. I tread lightly with it also because I am getting in the habit of enjoying life that I don't want to cut things short, but so many things happen. I don't seem to understand like a little accident last week that caused me considerable trouble and a night in the hospital and it was so subtle, the way it happened. As for as BA is concerned, I am glad for that one. I don't think I would be writing this letter. even now without the courage and action that I have had since' she' got out. So I'll expect only the best from everything that turns up and until it proves otherwise, I will consider it good.

I don't know just how we will decide to work it. I guess a tape recorder would be best for me to get. As for a time, I would prefer that we didn't set a regular hour until we have talked out all the details. I am very enthusiastic about this. I just wish I had more education now but I don't feel like waiting until I have a degree, there are so many things I have plans for in the future that I guess the next few years will pass very rapidly. I made a copy for myself so, unless something turns up from a " mood" you can keep this. I will do so in the future. And if you look over anything in the future that I wish returned I will indicate that on the front and avoid the embarrassment of asking you for them back Sincerely Bernice

> The cutting of the strings that bind
> A soul to another soul.
> It is painful. More hurt than
> Any eye can see,
> But I am impatient to be free.
> I bleed a little it is true,
> Each time I snip a string in two,
> I must do this, I must I must
> And somehow still not lose my trust.
> Oh god, you've heard me cry for help
> And sent to me your wisest one,
> Once more, I cry again for aid,
> To help me leave him unafraid.

Two nights ago, a strange thing happened while we were sleeping. It is so strange to relate, that I don't know if I can tell it or not. I was almost asleep. Please don't mistake this for a dream. It used to happen before we ever came to you.. Remember, the odd spiraling process we use to complain about. When we were sort of ripped apart from the body? Different ones experienced it, Now for convenience we will just say we, ,all right? We were aware that we had been slowly spiraled outside the body. We were perhaps in the body... We had no feeling of the body... It grows completely numb, like a foot asleep, only, this is the entire body... Even the face and fingers, everything.

We are aware of her. It is almost as if we were being allowed to see through her eyes. Maybe not allowed... Maybe forced to see through them. I know we were afraid. We were very very much afraid. It was as if she knew we were afraid. She had control. We were her guests, as it were. We saw her thoughts. . .. Not herself, we must have been somehow there together... But she was calm, that I know, and we were scared and "dead" and seeing what she wanted us to see. There also were men. All kinds, rough looking ones, kind looking ones, ugly bearded ones and good-looking ones. We sort of moved in and out among them, or they passed before us... I have no idea why this spectacle. They were just sitting or standing motionless. Not one word was spoken by the men or by her it was so still and weird that we were very shaken by the experience. We struggled for air and got back to our rightful place. We were trembling as we did during the week after we last saw you. I failed to mention then how when we were feeling better and our thoughts were calm and sensible that suddenly we would start shaking all over, arms and hands literally twitching and facial muscles in a jerking that we could not stop. We would climb back into bed if we were up and hold our arms and hands we to try to stop the tremor. We would climb back in bed if we were up to try to stop the tremor. Usually the tremor would end in the rigid condition I described earlier. Anyway, after awakening and realizing what had happened, we wanted to pass it off as a dream, but knew that it wasn't.

Today, Sunday 25th, has been a good day, about 1:30 we began to get drowsy and feel like we were drifting off or fading out. Just to be on the safe side, we came into the bedroom, and after a quick shower, we laid down to see if we could gather ourselves into a more alert state of mind. I last looked at the clock about 2 p.m. and awakened at 2:15 pm. So at the most a quarter of an hour was involved. We had another of those experiences and wrote down the following as rapidly as possible, but it still took 15 minutes to scribble it down. We were shaking like a leaf. And it was a full hour before the pulse settled and the system felt normal again.

This is a true copy(Ruth)

I'm afraid. Write this quickly. I couldn't move. The one who really is dangerous had the body. It was too strange. We all felt so numb and cold. Yes, numb. We could'nt move at all. It was no dream, was real. I felt, and I heard. Dark and very strange. It wanted to move about, said something like "come with me. I said

Ruth:"where? Where to?"

She: "Man. A certain man."

Ruth: "why"

She: "I'll_____him" (don't know if she said, drag, kill or what, I felt the purpose was not good. I was very scared)

I felt so strange and numb, the hands moved a little,. The body struggled to get up but couldn't. I was reluctant to move with it, maybe that's why I didn't get up completely. . I asked. "Do you know who I am?

" She answered quickly, "yes, Ruth"

Ruth: "what man are you looking for?"

She: "where is he?"

Ruth: "who?" (I kept wishing Dr. Young was here, but I was afraid to think it because she might want to hurt him)

She: "Glen"

Ruth: "I don't know anyone with the name to Glen.

" She: ", Glen and Lucy"

Ruth: "no. I don't know."

She: "he always took Lucy to the ranch. You know Glenn.

" Ruth: "I can't think. I don't know."

She: "in Wyoming."

This was at the end of the page. There was not another page.

(Ruth). I have been with her three times since yesterday morning in the last 24 hours, I could say. We decided to try and see if we can reach that one if we made an effort. Anne felt we did not have to be afraid too much, since always we have been able to leave her before she mobilized the body. We must not leave this one in this condition for something bad might happen. It could be disastrous for all of us. We also must repeat her wishes not to see Dr. Y.. I wish more than anything that we could talk to him, but we don't dare call him, somewhere in my mind I think that it would be all right if he contacted us.

2p.m..Yesterday afternoon about 2 p.m, II closed the house up and lay down with the deliberate intention of trying to "find " her. I'm glad that all of myself operated wonderfully. Roxanne was afraid, so we took some time first of all to get her to sleep. Everyone else worked with me. We thought we had better be united to make sure wc had proper strength to keep control. It took a little while to get through. We thought ourselves into a similar trance as came spontaneously yesterday. So we were "dead" except for awareness. She was there, nothing at all happened. I tried to think to her but there was no response at all. We couldn't wait very long as we needed air and had to come back into the body.

10:30 p.m..

I slept for a short time, and awakened. Was very relaxed and went to try to find her again. (The afternoon was depressing. We felt so alone. Bernas cried a little. The writer wrote a poem that was a statement of desolation. Anne was restless and in need of action, Nancy and Captain were trying to look ahead, Roxanne was still sleeping. Where is the dreamer now? No word from her for some time.).

I have in mind becoming adept at contacting the one that we fear. If we ever go to see Dr. Young again, we can use all the time working, without loss of time trying to find her. She came out fairly soon, we went out, whichever it is She moaned and struggled. I asked why and received no answer except we watched, felt in a lot of pain.

She seemed to be suffering. There was a body image and her teeth were being extracted. (So often we have had dreams of oral pain and loss of teeth). The teeth were being pulled out ,some whole, some in splintery fragments. It hurt. She struggled to get up. Blood seemed to be running all over her face and gasping for air. I think we couldn't take it any longer. We woke up and felt surprised that there was actually no blood at all. We had felt the warm wetness of blood, and seen it just a moment ago.

NowTuesday 7 a.m..

Mark went to work. We feel rough. Lay back down. Drifted without trying to and had numbness again. She said nothing but opened her eyes. We feel badly, said nothing. She said nothing. We want the doctor to help us. I need someone outside to help me talk to her. We can't let go, to talk. Struggle for air .We're back, and don't feel well.

Saturday

I will stay in this room, in this bed, without food until the whole self is dead. I have no place to live in this world. I do not belong. No one needs me. There is no hope. This man does not love me. I do not love him. I do not wish to see him or cook his food or wash his socks. I do not want to go somewhere with him. I do not want to talk to him. I only want to be left alone. He did not be very nice to me when I loved him. He would not even talk to me. He would not take me somewhere with hIm. He would be cross all the time. I was afraid of him. Now I hate him very much.

He called me Old Woman, and I wasn't. So that is why I will not live at all, if I have to live with him. Now I am very tired of not having any place to live, and I'm tired of hiding. I would rather be dead. He still does not want me and now I do not want him. I'm sick of him. And that is the truth.

Thursday the 15 ..

It's not very nice to say, you will do things like that to people. I hate things you say. I don't want tubes in my throat. Oh no. Why am I so weak? Because I'm dead mostly only the devil makes me a lie, but I can't stand up good. Why do you tell lies like that? I would use a gun instead of a rope. No one must find me to put tubes in my throat. He is not her friend either. I have no friend. He lies, and that's bad too. They are fools too. They think he is a friend. I'll find a place to die well. I'll take off the face. Then they can't see me anymore. I don't want people to look at me, either. I'm dead and they know it. I don't want to go to sleep. I'm afraid. It's too lost and too bad. I have no friend. People are not trustable. I don't sleep. I won't let anyone put tubes in my throat again. I'll scream, and I will too. I'll bite. I'll hit real hard. I want to go back and be dead again.

Hello Dr.

I (Anne) and myself have thought over things we discussed Tuesday. We felt that you were right. Well, we don't need you or any other doctor, BF, BW and Roxanne are far from well. Now we were under a great deal of pressure to stop seeing you, and the pressure was lifted immediately when we made a decision to stop. And when there was a decision to continue therapy, it brought a deluge of powerful emotions that soon knocked me right out the picture. I lost the evening and night. I did wake this morning, and I was quiet inside.

Mike said she or whatever it was, was dead set on suicide. The attitudes I pick up on paper have a common theme. "He went into deep water with us and then left us to drown." He went back to safety, and now stands on the bank laughing while we sink." I know this isn't true and you know it isn't, but the problem is, can you do anything as long as that attitude prevails? I can probably get the body there and turn it over to you, but I can't force them to accept you in good faith. If they have no confidence in you, I can try to influence them in your favor as I had been doing, but I cannot guarantee I will succeed but I will try to do what is best, at least with" myself" and I'm going to remain positive. I'm not unwilling, but inside there's a great protest and the protest comes from the source of infection. If you care to work against such odds then I will cooperate. The attitude of my little friends inside will no doubt give me a bad time, but it looks sometimes like a bad time is inevitable from time to time anyway. But if I have a choice of living with bad attitudes or dying with them. I'd rather live with them, because they are still an unsettled part of me.

P.S. If you think it worthwhile to try, My new hours when I am free for any morning to at 11 o'clock and from three on in the afternoon. If I have to miss a class I will come or if you want to try two hour stretches that will be okay.

Dear Dr. Young.

I'm writing this out of fear that you might become discouraged now we are working with this last development, and I don't want you to. It is true that I have so much anxiety when I come to your office now that

I can hardly communicate at all. Certainly not enough to give you any encouragement that you are helping at all.

I took the liberty of taking a capsule of Librium after all. I decided that I had better have confidence in your judgment, and it was all right. It was to my benefit that I did. I was anxious all morning, not when I spoke with you. I went to sleep shortly after taking the capsule and awakened in less than an hour, completely clear and refreshed, so I see now that you are right.

I hope you can remember that the one you are working with now is not all I am, and does not express the hope and confidence I also feel. I am looking forward to being a complete and real person someday including this part because I can't be a "whole" person and have some of me missing. Maybe my ambitions for life are too great and I'll find I can't accomplish as much as I would like to once I do find myself on stable ground, but I suppose it is for sure we will never fly beyond our goals. So, if they are too far to reach, we might still fly farther than if we had no ambitions or goals at all. Right now, I do feel discouraged often, but my only real fault lies in the one you are dealing with now (which I think must be the last) in my mind. Of course, if it isn't the last and it is added to what I have already gained, I will be even more strong to face another part if there is more. All I really wanted to say is please don't be offended or discouraged by this one. I know it is pessimistic, and not very polite, but I still keep thinking. well, whatever it is this is part of me. So I want the best possible done with it and if you can't find anything good in it as you did the rest of us, maybe if you can help it decide to live, it can share whatever good the rest of us possess. I am sure someday, not too far off, we will be able to be more useful than we are now and able to move about with other people without feeling so overwhelmed by life. I hope so, respectfully, Ruth and all of us

The theme, "I don't care." It's not altogether self-pity and you can call it what you want, but I do know the whole truth and I think it is a mixture of self-pity, self-doubt lack of trust in others, and a complete feeling a uselessness. No one can dispute the fact that we are useful at home most of the time anyway, and if we aren't doing anything, we are at the least, a symbol of a mother to the kids. But this isn't really enough; maybe because we often have to demand respect from the children; also, we know the girls can do anything as well as we can now, except coordinate and supervise the home and family. This too is a not appreciated role as naturally enough, kids don't appear to want to be supervised or coordinated.

I keep trying to find some place we are a needed. Some volunteer work is done mostly by people only in clubs. While some good does come from these I'm sure, there is too much formality and too little actual active work. We have not learned to do anything unless it has a purpose so it is difficult to just "enjoy life." We are so critical. We have a pioneer spirit, and no courage to use or no place to apply it. At least no place we have found yet. Now I am still looking for an outlet that is constructive and to write some every day. 2000 to 3000 words but the ideas seemed to begin to look pretty shoddy.

I can't cope with this any longer. I'm tired of the hope followed by disappointment. I can't see anything for me beyond the routine, a housewife,-mother, and that I can't face. I am kidding myself when I dream of a place in life with other people, yet I can't, I don't want this. I can't live just for my kids, but what else is there? Oh yes, the world is big and full of opportunity, but I don't fit anywhere, I don't belong anywhere. I have tried. I tried so hard. I don't think I have any more incentive to try. And the school isn't the answer. I might study until I had a doctor's degree. I've no doubt that I could, but what good would it do me? I can't even face a small crowd of people without trembling inside? When I am so tired and unhappy inside that I spend my time alone and cry? I wish I could be of some use in the world. I could help someone worse than myself. The only people that need me are tiny babies and they all have mothers. I have no value unless I am contributing something to life. But how? To exist just to be living, to be happy just to be alive is impossible for me. I can be happy with my dreams, with my books, but what I'm constantly being called on is happiness, and I can't be with other people because I don't fit. I tried it, I know I write the truth. To stay alive10 years more to make a home for my kids, to maybe save them from the few difficulties. is this the only reason? That's not enough. All I can do for them is to make life very convenient with food, shelter and fresh clothing and stand aside after that, wait around with the hope that they might need encouragement or advice, and by the time they do, I am so discouraged myself that I'm hardly fit to give it. I want to be different, I want to change, but how can I when every attempt I make to mingle with others is a failure. If I could do just anything to succeed, if I could be useful outside of these four walls, or could be satisfied within them.

.

Dr. Yong.

- You seem to have forgotten that I exist, but I do exist and have always existed. I watched every move, every mistake, incorrect moves you have made in relation to myself. I have evaluated as well as I could since that is my capacity. You once referred to me as the evaluator. I don't give a darn what you call me. I stopped myself from seeing you, I allowed myself to come back again. Mostly I couldn't find anyone else to do the work as you do. I become weary of the fght, sometimes I think it best to die. This has been a hard week, we are still here. I don't want to die any more than does anyone else, but I want to live, not exist. I've been thinking maybe I have misjudged you partly. I don't know. This one, who I have held down for so long is a block of trouble. I have had you pegged as a religious person who would approve of such a creature who thanks God every day for the privilege to draw another breath with which to suffer for others. she dutifully submits to every obstacle in life and calls it God's will. So I felt it especially necessary to keep her away from you. For a while, I thought you might do but I changed my mind after you and Anne made perfect fools of yourselves. Now she is so near out of control that we might as well level and get all the cards on the table. I have decided recently, after a few visits to go to another doctor, but that we might as well have a final-round, as the stakes are high, to let you talk to her as you felt you had found the "lost soul" and if you attempted to restore it to the fold as leader, then I could stop things pronto and not with pills or anything else so unreliable. If things come to death it would be sure. We'll use a gun, and I won't spill blood on her clean floor, not because I care for the mess, but because I would respect the children enough not to have them find the equivalent of a headless horseman. I sound brutal, but I think some things are more brutal. While God may give life I also think he might give us a new start. We might do better next time. Instead of thinking of suicide as an unseemly thing, I think it might be the same as a return to God and saying: "I goofed this time, but I'd like to try again. Maybe with what I learned at this time on earth, I'll be able to make a good deal out of the next try". One has to have some sense enough to know when to quit sometimes too and give up a task that isn't practical. We are not easy, but I don't apologize for that.

- Since you did talk to her and tend to not feel that she is it, then I have felt a little more hope that you might do. But there isn't room for too many more mistakes, so I would like to help you keep from making any more than is necessary. For one thing, we do have to hurry. Someway we must find something to do. I don't know if there is anything you can do about that except offer some encouragement. We can do something. You have read this page. You see that there is energy that must be used. There is a need to be and feel useful. You might as well say "drop dead", as to say wait until you are well and then worry about doing something. We won't get well, unless we do something. It is as necessary as oxygen. Your main job is to try to make that "nice" Mrs. Brown see how prudish it is to try to be as agreeable as Mike's mother. She isn't his mother. I'm doing my best to believe you'll be honest, and play fair. Of all things, I hate insincerity. So please don't lie. If you feel she is right about something, I will respect you more if you say so. I mean, that just because I say she has to change, that doesn't mean that you encourage change where you feel things are alright. As I said before, be honest, I would prefer you saying flatly. "Go to hell" than to have you beat around the bush trying to balance things. I don't consider that I have been dishonest with you by keeping Mrs. B .hidden, after all ,a person has a right to decide whether a doctor is to be trusted or not. And I'm not so sure as yet about you. Maybe you can and maybe you can't. You can be trusted to do what you think is best ,it's just that you don't know what's best. But even worse is the fact that there isn't any other doctor I've found who knows as much as you do or who is flexible enough to be trained (excuse the egoism). I only mean but at least you will on occasion listen to my advice, and after all they are my people, so I know more of what I want done with them. I don't want them deceived.

He hates me now, I know he does. He has been such a liar such a deceiver. He thinks I don't know how unwelcome I am in his room. He hasn't time to call because I'm not important. If one wants to do something he does it. I'm always so sleepy and tired because I never feel rested. I hate the housework. But I'm not important enough for anything else. Why should she have books to read but never for me? They have all thought I'm too stupid to read a book. It's just because I have too much housework to do. And my feet swell and my hands swell, but that's alright. My blood pressure isn't important at all. I'm very jealous of them all. And that's bad, but why am I so different? Why should no one call me and say how are you? You never ask how I am. I don't feel very good. And I don't want to sew those dresses because she would wear them anyway. I know I'm very bad, I know that. I don't care if I am. Someday when I'm not tired., I'll find it very quiet place to sleep. I'm tired of caring for children too. There's much confusion in my mind, but only her troubles are important. I'm selfish and bad."

I couldn't get any coordination yesterday after she wrote this.

I just can't find the strength for living. I know I must have some potential for good and for happiness, if I can find it and go to bed. I'm so lonely. I do try, I really do try hard, but this vast loneliness rises inside of me and I am afraid. I have been sleeping so little and I just seem to have lost the spirit or desire for living. I don't think I'm such a coward altogether, but sometimes we just have to have sense enough to know when to stop, and it must be about time for me. I can't survive. Or maybe I just no longer want to survive it alone. I'm counting on you to understand. Thanks for all you did and try to do for me, Bernice.

(doctor'snote)

I was concerned that this might be a suicide note. I had been thinking about the one who complained about her teeth being extracted and also about tubes being put in her throat. I had what I believed was an understanding of the situation and decided to move at this time to make an intervention. I had my secretary contact Bernice and arrange an appointment. I asked my secretary to tell her that I had decided how to help and to not give up.

When Bernice came in, I explained to her the following: "I have been thinking about the one that complains about her teeth being extracted and about tubes being put in her throat. I don't know if this is from one or two sources of consciousness. I believe I've figured out what has happened and how to correct it. My plan is to tell her that I'm a talking doctor, which means I only talk and do not do anything that hurts. I think that she is able to make herself numb since you feel feel numb when you're talking to her and maybe she can feel no pain when she does that. When I talk to her, I will tell her I believe she became aware during operations in which the operation was not protected by an anesthetic to her level of consciousness and she woke up and she did not understand what was happening because she was not conscious when the operations were planned and approved by you. Can you imagine what it would be like to wake up with someone extracting your teeth without your permission? I appreciate your trust in coming to me for help with this. I think we can do it with very little risk and the benefits are very much worth it. I notice that you have not asked if I suggested this problem and I think we have gained some trust. Are you ready to do this?"

"Yes. I trust you. Go ahead."

"Close your eyes and relax. I will count for you to go down to the beach. You can listen to this if you want to since you are working with her already, I counted to 10,then I asked to talk to this one. "Somewhere in your mind, you woke up to having someone pulling out your teeth. I think you are able to make yourself numb. I want you to make yourself numb now so you will not feel any pain. I am a talking doctor. I only talk. You do not need to be afraid of me. I will not do anything, to cause any pain. I just want to talk to you and explain something. I don't think you understood what was happening to you. All I am asking you to do is to listen while I explain what happened. Your teeth had so many cavities that your conscious mind, Bernice, was having a great amount of pain from toothaches. It is possible that you did not feel the pain or know why your teeth were being taken out because you are able to make your body to feel numb. Bernice decided to have all the teeth removed and have dentures, false teeth, fitted for her mouth. She arranged for a dental surgeon to remove the teeth. I think you must not have become conscious of this and that is why you must have been very surprised, when you woke up and found out your teeth were being removed without your consent. I understand how frightening and distressing that must've been for you. I think whatever the doctor did to keep your conscious mind from feeling the pain of the extractions did not protect you from feeling your teeth being pulled out. You became conscious that your teeth were being removed, and did not understand why this was happening and also felt a great deal of pain. I can understand how frightening that must've been. I think that now when you become conscious, you feel the memory of the pain, and you do not know that the mouth has healed and is not painful any more. Your mouth has healed now and is not causing any pain.

Someway we must help you find that out. You need to be able to feel your mouth without any pain from it now. You have false teeth in your mouth now. The first thing I want you to do is to feel is your face. You have felt that there is blood on your face. I want you to take your hand and feel your face. You will find there is no blood on it. Okay, you are feeling your face and there is no blood on it. Now put your fingers in your in your mouth and feel the teeth that are there. You feel the false teeth that have replaced the teeth that were removed. Your mouth has healed up. Now don't expect to feel pain when you feel your jaw now. Good, the pain is gone. I hope you can see that I am helpful and do not cause you pain. I expect that because you had the experience of someone pulling out your teeth without your consent that you may have had a distrust of people or doctors. This was a misunderstanding, because you were not conscious when the consent was given. I hope this clears up the misunderstanding and you can be trustful of people now.

There is something else that needs to be explained. There was an operation on your throat because they thought you had a cancer of the thyroid gland. I have read what you wrote about that you didn't want straws, which were tubes, put in your throat .You woke up and didn't know why they were putting tubes in your throat. I can understand why you were so angry about this, because you had no knowledge of why this was being done or knowledge of consent. This was very frightening .I would have been angry too if I woke up, and somebody was putting tubes in my throat without me knowing why and not knowing I had given a consent. This was a terrible misunderstanding and caused you to be angry at and distrustful of people. I want you to know that the operation on your neck was done because they thought you had a cancer but fortunately it was not cancer. After the lump was removed, the doctor put a tube or two in the incision to drain any fluid that is produced so it would not be in the way of the wound healing up. After the healing has begun the doctor takes the tubing out. The wound has healed now and the tubing is gone. I want you to be able to know what is going on outside. You need to be awake with the rest of your mind so you know what is happening, You may be afraid of knowing what is happening or pushed out of awareness because you are fearful. I want you to become able to trust Bernice to know which people are trustworthy, to make good decisions about what to do. The rest of your mind can help you learn to do that. They are not fools, and are smart and do guard for your safety and your rights. Your ability to make yourself numb is useful when you are hurt and need to be numb and block the pain until you are well again. You need to remain aware so you can know when the problem is fixed, and you can turn your feeling back on again.

It was also reported to me that there was a feeling of being unable to get any air when your other selves joined with you and I think that being unable to breathe may have been because someone assisting in the operation was controlling your breathing. You should not have trouble breathing now. You can have control of your brething .

I hope this will help you. The rest of yourself wants to work with you and have you join them in living a safe and happy life. If they feel a need for my help, I hope you feel you don't need to be afraid of me and I will be as helpful as I can. Let me speak with Ruth. Goodbye now.

Ruth, you trusted me enough to bring your selves in. I hope what I have done will help.. I am very pleased that you are being very helpful with the rest of yourself and have been helpful with this one , (or two?) who's been in such pain and distrust of others. You are not only living, you're taking an active part in making things better. It has taken courage for you and the rest of yourself to work with this self on your own and also to bring her to me for assistance. I know you did not think you should need any help for your mind but sometimes it helps to have a" mind mechanic", when it isn't a car that needs fixing. I would not expect you to know what was wrong for this part of yourself and how to straighten out the misunderstanding. So, I hope you are not going to lose any self-esteem or courage, when you could not fix it yourself and asked for my help. I commend you and your selves for trying what you did being able to know and ask for assistance when you needed it. It must have been very scary to trying to help her when you could not get any air and were very numb all over. You are all very brave.

I want to say to all of you that I know how it feels to find when you think this is the last thing that needs to be done and you find out there is more. I have found out it is not endless and that if you keep on going you do finally get to the finish, but it is sometimes long and frustrating. Don't give up. You have learned by now, that something can be done about it and you have gained some experience in doing it yourself.

The following was written by hand by someone identified by herself in this writing as "the dreamer". At the first she drew seven concentric circles, each larger than the next.. She began with a small one inside, which was numbered !(one).

Below this, she wrote. "I. a most wonderful child-sensitive, intelligent, and quite healthy physically.

2. A preschooler, whose security was threatened by many things, A. unhappy family B. incompatible parents C. to break up in a family through father's behavior with Gertie. D. ignorance of culture which promoted scary tales with fears of the dark ,snakes, insects, thunder and lightning fearfulness encouraged. Resources: an imagination and ability to create fantasies which made world tolerable and gave escape.

3.Age 4 to-6 illness and death of mother, a-mad mule,-boy killed by horse, the death of one of Gerties daughters who caught her clothes on fire and died before Gertie married father,-stepmother, ,Gertie,of a Cinderella type stepmother, expulsion from home= rejection so great that all former fears were intensified and security shaken. Result= the trauma or closing off= separating of this part of life= leaving a hollow shell in a hostile environment=.Resources: imagination= ability to create a dream world, which made years more tolerable when dependence on others, was necessary and not available.

4.Adolescence: attempting to "grow up" and become independent. The dreams and fantasies were no longer appropriate. They were un realistic as environment became less sheltered. Never never land.

5. Running for shelter again via a marriage, looking for early security, unable to give and receive. Dreams and make believe still indulged in, but not suitable for adult role in life.

6. Conflict. Trying to care for offspring in adult role, while still being a scared child within brought illness. Dreams stifled _never never land.

7, Years spent trying to become a person through various channels. Therapy education, redesigning life through divorce, working among people, remarriage ,some success much success really due to some insight gained through therapy. Thought, reading and experiences gained. Dreamer still helping Still the most wonderful part of person. Most potential sees great need to uncover ,recover and integrate parts 1 2 and 3 with rest of self.

The adult Bernice must accept the child and all things that made up the early Bernas. Must give up ill-gotten gains to original owner. Must allow Bernas to live for only through her can the child become alive again. The dreamer can see these things clearly. It is not a dream. It is true that Bernas had the right and must live.

A strong outside helper is needed Doctor Y must be more interested and persistent, or his value is little. He should be forceful in demanding that the child be uncovered and that Bernas live. I say from my position inside that it is not right for Bernas to be allowed to "choose" if she goes to sleep or not. She's stopping progress. She will stop therapy completely. I speak with authority of one who sees it all. Dr. Young could be the only hope there is, for he knows there is trouble. He must be strong and not fear Bernice, If he does work with the inner life, the dreamer will force her to come however loud she may protest. There is a life that is buried .Bernice is a shell without_, just a hard shell. The goodies are all inside and could be brought out. The shell could be like a form to hold them up. I wrote these things hoping you can know, I understand, and hoping you will be stronger. I believe in my dreams, and think quite well of my productions. I wish to share my ego and find expression for all of my inside views. Must not be sold short or treated as insignificant. I rest my case and yeald the floor to the good doctor to see if he will proceed with real intent. I fight for my inner world by pleading thus."

Below this was written in a different, scrawling, handwriting:"rubbish all this is rubbish. She tries to think like a person. She isn't a person only a shadow, an escaped prisoner."

On the same type of paper in the handwriting of the main writing above was the following:

1._1929-1934: Roxanne also known as The Little Girl-_-The Ghost (. Possibly the infant?) The child, Nancy.

2.__ 1934 1936 Bernas. In the outer world _Alienated from The child ,Birmingham ,Grenades chapel Enterprise__ Nancy visited.__

1936 1942 Bernice developed from Bernas a mixture with Bernas an attempt to adjust. Nancy visited

4'__ 19421946 Bernice, adolescence, Rock Springs, still strong blending.

5.__ Bernice__-Bernas schism more acute.

6._Bernice-Bernas-Civil War begins.

7.__ Bernice has illness, shadows of past and the ghost of Roxanne attempt to live and compete in a complex world. Nancy comes back off and on.

I replied to the dreamer:

Dear dreamer:

Thank you for your letter. Your insight will be very helpful. I will use the information in your suggestions. Since you have contact with much of yourself, you may be able to work with the others to accomplish the changes, which you suggest. See what you can do to make a difference. I appreciate that you bring into focus areas of concern by dreams and other means of conveying information.

Sincerely, Dr. Young.

After a visit, Bernice or other, wrote a note in which she was angry about something I had said. This had frequently happened. My words and my meaning were misunderstood. She said. "I hate for you for saying I am bad. I would not mind admitting I'm divided, if I could believe you would not proceed to use it to prove I'm crazy. If there is any way I can alter my attitude, tell me."

Since all I had told her and done, had not changed this fearful distrust, I decided to search for the origin of this attitude. When she came for her next appointment, I told her my plan.

"Bernice, you wrote that if there was a way you could alter your attitude, I should tell you, I have thought about this and I believe the attitude arises from something that happened in the past. I want to see if I can find the source and change it. I am going now to search for the source. Please close your eyes and return to the beach, which you can now do more quickly than before. So that when I count to three, You'll be sitting at the beach again. One, two, three. Now you're at the beach, ignore what I'm saying until I call for you. I want to speak to your mind and ask for you to search for some were that you are afraid of being called crazy. You are afraid of being called crazy, and I want to tell you something important. I do not think you are crazy. I am a mind doctor and I know whether someone is crazy or not. You are not crazy, and I'm not going to say you are. Why are you afraid of being called crazy?"

"Gertie said I was crazy. She told Popa I was crazy, because I talked to Nancy and she talked to me. She said I was crazy because I talked to my dolls and they talked to me .Papa told me to stop talking to Nancy. She told him to not let me take my dolls when he sent me with my sister. She said I was crazy. I am not crazy. She said I was bad and Popa sent me away. I hate her."

I replied:;Gertie was ignorant and did not know what she was talking about. Children do have friends that are in their minds and they can talk with them. They're not crazy. I think they are very smart and you are too. You were a lonely child and you were able to have Nancy stay with you for company in your mind after she went home. You were also able use your dolls for company too. We call it having imaginary playmates, but they are not just imaginary because they're able to make them real inside their minds. I want you to stop being afraid that people are going to say you're crazy, because you're not and you can tell them that a wise mind doctor has said you are not crazy. But I don't think anybody is going to call you that, because they are not as stupid as Gertie. Because Gerti said all those bad things about you, you became afraid of what people would say about you. Most people are not as stupid and mean as Gertie was and if someone says mean things about you, you just say they are stupid and ask your inside friend, Anne,who can help you tell them off if they do not believe when you explain what I have told you., She's good at telling people off if they say stupid things about you. I am a doctor who understands these things about how the mind works and you do not have to be afraid I will say you are crazy. I will only say good things about you because I know you are not crazy. Whatever I say, I want you to expect it to be good and understand it is a good thing I'm saying about you. Will you believe these good things I've said about you?"

"yes, you are a good doctor like Dr. Middleton. Thank you."

Remember the things I have told you. You can talk to your friends inside your head now, without feeling you are crazy when you do it. They will help you feel better and help you take care of yourself. You can talk to yourself now without being afraid of being caked crazy. We will wait a few minutes while you talk to your self."

Bernice, you can wake up now and talk to me. Stretch now and come into focus. I have talked to a part of your mind that was called crazy by Gertie whom I would say Gertie was the crazy one because she thought she was the authority and that she knew Bernas was crazy because Bernas heard Nancy and her dolls talk to her and Bernas talked to them, which really did happen in her mind. Gertie did not understand this. She told her Papa previously to tell Bernas to stop talking to Nancy and her dolls and to not let her take her dolls with her to Birmingham This is the source of one of the "troubles" in Bernas's sack full of troubles. She became afraid of being called crazy if she said she heard voices. And I think she is the source of your fear that I would say you were crazy If you had acknowledged that you do hear your selves talk to you. I assured her that that would not happen and that Gertie did not know what she was talking about and was stupid and that I was an authority about who was crazy, and who was not crazy and that she is not crazy. I told her that children often have imaginary playmates and are able to hear them talk and that is a normal thing. I told her Gertie was wrong and she was right, because she could really hear them from inside her head . She just didn't realize where the voices were coming from. I hope this will help you be able to accept your alter personalities without fearing that you will be called crazy. Let us see if you can do that now."

"I will think about telling you they are real and see if I feel okay doing that."(Pause) "It works I don't feel scared about saying I can hear my selves talk to me."

"Good , now, you can communicate with yourself without feeling frightened and without fear of talking about it to selected people who can understand that this does not mean that you are crazy."

"Thank you. I feel freer now. I'll see you next week."

Some important changes had been made in Bernice's life at this time. She had decided to do postgraduate work in social services and I had heartily recommended her to the Social Service Department of the College, and she is now in the social services program.

She has met and married Larry who is a well-educated, social worker, who loves Bernice knowing and accepting her with her multiple personalities, and he is very supportive and devoted. I told Bernice that she had married a commoner at first but now Cinderella had her prince at last. Although her treatment was not completed, she had accomplished very much, as is indicated in the next segment.

One problem comes up after another, and you hope that you have resolved the last one in the tote bag on the back of Bernas. But sometimes there is a pleasant surprise. On the above date, I received a 17 page handwritten pleasant surprise. The author of the information began with numbered concentric circles previously reported, added more. She provides a greater insight about the internal condition and the experiences contributing to her circumstances. Her contribution is as follows:

For many years I've heard my children cry inside, and sometimes laugh. I felt their hurt and their joy, their fear, but most of all, perhaps, I've sensed their great longing and loneliness for something left behind. I have experienced the helplessness and frustration of their alienation and felt my adult body wracked with half choked sobs and trembling fears. But life goes on for many souls whose life was shattered as mine was. And now that much pain is relieved, I'm so glad that I'm alive, that painful death wishes did not win. I know I was only half alive before I knew my little ones. And now I live in many ways I've never lived before, and the end is not yet, not yet.

I came just now from Dr. Young's office, how many visits in the past and how many hours. I don't know for a while ago I stopped keeping track. It just isn't important, nor is the years it took. The important thing is that I have begun to understand, to know my children and, yes, to live.

My neck is stiff today and ,when I woke up in the big chair, my face wet with tears. At first the dreadful choking feeling was in my throat, but it went quickly as I became more fully awake, and the neck tension lingers yet but not so much. I can remember faintly, a conversation today. He talked with my crippled little girl I think of as Patti Jo. I'm not sure it is yet, that it is her, but somehow, I believe it is, for Patti Jo was a timid child. Dr. Young is a good man, a good doctor. He is patient and kind, and he coaxed words from the child taught a long while ago to be forever silent,-not forever! (for she may yet talk).

(The following was marked out). I felt a deep sadness and fear, as she had felt so many years ago, and a choking.)

We began our session with a bit of small talk, he had just returned from his vacation, and yet we kept the small talk down for time is precious , a 50 minute hour. I had hoped he would continue working with the little girl lost in the woods. But he insited ,asked for the one who wanted to keep quiet. She awoke, but reluctantly, for she does not wish to be noticed. It is better, she explained, to be quiet, because we aren't supposed to say anything."

"why not? Why must you always be quiet?" He asked.

"Because, because we aren't supposed to say anything." And the choking deepened and the tension increased. The voice is timid and unsure. A sense of fear so great, I know that little scared girl would prefer the doctor to stop talking too, because he was calling attention to her and she wished to be unnoticed. But doctor knows enough history to know which buttons to press."

"Someone told you to be quiet and play?"

"Well yes, but I really should,"

"You should? Why do you think you should ? Did someone tell you to be quiet?"

"Papa yelled at me. He said to be quiet. Didn't I know my mother was dying? I wasn't making any noise. My cousin was. I felt very bad, because my mother was dying, and Papa was so angry at me. I have got to be quiet."

"You do not have to be quiet forever. Your mother was dying then and it was your cousin and not you who was making a noise. You can be free to talk new. Are there other times you've been told to be quiet?"

"yes. When I lived with my sister and Herman they told me to be quiet all the time. They told me to shut up. They said children should be seen and not heard. When that they were talking, they told me not to interrupt."

Bernice comments: "I felt the old loyalty to those misguided souls who will like a dog, and lick the hand of the master who beats him. I taught myself to feel grateful for the abuse, and now all these years, even decades later, I feel loyalty.

" The little girl said:"They knew I wasn't important."

I defended my sister and her husband, who had taken me into their home, which was oppressed with poverty, enough already without a seven-year-old child to feed. Even now, I defend them, for I cannot believe they felt they were doing wrong. She was so young herself, my sister was just a teenager .A minimum age for marriage had never been heard of in our mountain community .My sister was 15 when she was married. If a girl was still unmerited at 16, there was a grave danger of becoming an old maid so my sister had married at 15 and escaped becoming a spinster and perhaps escaped an intolerable home life, though. I cannot be sure how things were for her, and she was a poor soul starved for love and cruel from the starvation impoverished so long and deprived. She looked at me with resentment, and intrusion, and the power she felt over me reached sadistic peaks at times. My sister herself was in a difficult position. Now, the care of an infant had been placed on her young shoulders and years before by a sick mother and her baby sister. And now the infant was again with her, but she did say, "be quiet" and felt this was her right to tell me to be quiet. See? See how I still defend her? This child within me feels guilty if I think of my sister and brother-in-law in any way except with gratitude.

But I had been already uprooted and unplanted and sent thousands of miles away to the city I both feared and detested and I had learned as a child of seven I was insignificant compared to the adult, so it was with a great meekness born of fear that quieted me, and I choked back words. Words of protest words of longing for Papa and for the weathered little house in the pines. I choked back questions of why. Why did I have to come here? Why must I eat my beans alone in the cold kitchen? Why must I be quiet always? Why do I have to mind the baby all the time and never join in the walks the two of you take together every evening? It gets dark in the house, and I am told not to light a lamp. "Just give the baby her bottle and stay with her and I would watch them go hand-in-hand, for they were emotionally attached at that time and the baby I loved anyway, so I stood by her crib and changed her diapers and walked to the door again and again hoping they would be coming back down the street before dark, for soon the baby would drink all her milk and I would be in the house alone and dusk would gather even though a street lights shone outside, I would be in the dark. I want to cry and shout "you know, I'm afraid of the dark. You know, I am for your remember how Papa left a light burning for me even if it was low. You know, and you do it on purpose, making me stay in the dark for so long with the baby. And the thoughts I pushed down, pushed so far down, because I knew that to live I must cooperate. I must be good. And I was trouble enough already, I have been told, without fussing about things, so I choked the words back and the tears were checked but the neck was stiff and rigid and the head hurt so much.-And when they came back, Herman would say as he always did. " You're just a scaredy-cat". Contempt would be in his voice, and he would look at me with hatred and say "look at yourself in the mirror and see what a dummy you are. Nobody would bother with you. You're so ugly. You'd scare off a nigger in the dark" and then he would snicker in his peculiar way of saying "hee hee hee " and his face would darken again, and he'd say, "you better mind me you dumbbell. I said look in the mirror" then he took a step toward me. I 'd look in the mirror and see what a dumbbell I was and I agreed. Yes, I was so ugly, so very plain. My face was shiny, and my eyes were too big. And my hair was oh so very straight. No dimples or curls like Shirley Temple for sure and when I was properly intimidated he would be satisfied and say "Now you git to bed and hurry up about it." and I'd hurry. I pulled my two quilts out of the closet spread one on the far side of the kitchen and covered up with the other. And then we go through the same routine, night after night. I would hope each time that I could get by without shutting the door myself. But then, his form would loom in the doorway, and he'd say "you dummy. You can't learn anything. You git out of bed and close this door. You can't remember anything. I've told you every dern night since you been here, to close the door. You can't remember anything." So I would get up and close the door. I hadn't forgotten it .It was just that I knew that once the door was closed there would be no more light in the kitchen except a small crack under the door. I would creep slowly over and close the door quickly and run, run fast back to my pallet and pulled the quilt quickly over my head. The dark was bad, but not so bad if your eyes were shut very tight and you were under the covers. The sobs that rose in my throat I would choke back, and be quiet because I dared not cry, ever again. I would just choke the sobs until they died inside. And I trembled, until I fell asleep. And that is how I learned to be quiet.

Learning to be quiet was perhaps necessary in some circumstances. I'm sure it did not help me in public, for I became so withdrawn, so actually convinced that I was evil and a perpetual problem that I must have given the appearance of being dimwitted.

School was soon to start in Birmingham, and I was ready for the third grade. Having covered the first and second my first school year. I could not tell the principal where I belonged for I was seven and he said second-grade. He was probably a reasonable man. I still remember what he looked like. He was youngish and very neat, but I do not remember his name. The school was large, so large. So many children pretty children well dressed children. Children who came holding tight to their mothers hand. Children who came in groups, smiling children laughing and noisy children, more children than I'd ever seen before in my life. Children plain but happy children ragged and a little dirty, but with a gleam of life in their eyes that made me fear them. I stayed close to the building, while on the playground, but I wasn't invisible. Children ran all around me, shouting rushing. A group of five of the girls, slightly older than me, roved around the school yard arm in arm, in pretty dresses bright shoes and well brushed curly hair. I wanted to look like them but was painfully aware of my high top laced shoes and a dress that was too short. I kept watching them and perhaps that's why they trooped over arm in arm. They formed a semi circle around me. I had only the cold brick wall behind me. "What's your name?" They chanted.

"Bernas, Bernas"
one said.
"That's a funny name. What grade are you in?"
"Second"
"Second-grader. Second-grader!
She's a fraider! She's a fraider!"
Oh those dear little girls. Had I smiled had I been brave, they might have been my friends (I wonder where they are today, matrons like myself with grown children may be even grandchildren perhaps). But I wasn't brave and I didn't smile, and so they chanted. "Bernas Bernas built a furnace second-grader she's a fraider" and others joined them and I was still and cold against the brick wall and then, oh wonderful sound!, literally saved by the bell , I was. And my tormentors ran to be the first in line, and

I was all too glad to bring up the rear. I remembered Audrey Hodgins, the little redheaded girl, who back in Rising Fawn was always last in line. I had felt so superior to her only last spring, and now I had fallen in the ranks and would gladly have clasped her hand.

The classroom of the second grade was a haven after the playground. We sat at little tables by fours. Two girls and two boys. The little boy on my side of the table was very shy, and the little blond girl was also quiet. On the other side of the table, a fat little boy named Junior, who wore green short pants and a shirt every day, sat across from me and I liked my table. I liked the room. I liked the books we were given and the blackboard with colored paper balloons taped across the top. I liked the long rows of windows, which were to be decorated at Christmas time. I liked Miss Middleton, the tall skinny teacher who wasn't too young or too old and who spoke kindly to me.

The morning passed and again we were turned into the playground, a virtual nightmare. One could not hide. We were supposed to play and join in the games, but I lingered on the outskirts and tried to be inconspicuous.

My morning walks to school were a dreaded thing . Afternoons many children walked on the sidewalks. If the dogs barked there were other children, and although I walked alone I did not mind the dogs, and finally I would be on my street and then my steps would lag, for I was not too eager to go inside. But in the mornings, I walked alone and the dogs barked, and I cried inside. My little girl was so afraid that I would tell her beautiful stories and let her share my dreams. I taught her to shut out reality and to think her own thoughts and dreams I taught her to think of wonderful things. You could be ever so grand, ever so nice in a dream, even pretty. I would be her mother some mornings and at first I had to help her think of a mother. I would give her the image of myself, as a pretty lady. A lady who wore high heels and carried a purse in one hand and held her little hand in the other. Then I dressed her in my mind and made her think of pink dresses with ruffles and satin ribbons. I made her think of black shiny shoes and white socks and curls. She would go along beautifully with me until we reached the school and then she rubbed out my pretty thoughts and looked at the frightening scene around her of children, noise, chanting. She would forget the pink ruffles and believed in her old faded print dress like Cinderella. All the beauty would evaporate, and she stood barren of riches, scared, stiff and silent

Her work was good. She never made a mistakes and Miss Middleton noticed this and one day when the principal came in the little girl became painfully aware that they were talking about her. She was terrified. What had she done wrong?. Had Herman told them what a dummy she was? Or had she gotten in trouble for slipping behind the shrubbery out of sight on the play ground as she had taken to doing lately? Anyway, the teacher and the principal came for her, and he said. "Come with me." She went cold and scared and silently she followed down the hallway and through the corridor and into his office and still didn't know what she had done wrong . I tried to be her mother to hold her hand to make her feel pretty but she shut me out and sat on the big chair at the table and waited for the ax to fall ,so small and so cold and so very much alone." O papa when will you come for me? When can I go home?" But the tears did not come and the voice was not heard and the clock ticked loudly or the wall. The principal said : "You are too smart for the second grade. You're going to go into the third grade."

Bernice wrote: "Last night, one of my children cried. I don't know which one, but she cried and sobbed, and she was allowed to do so. The deep sobs came suddenly, shortly after we went to bed. We had had a pleasant evening, visited was some old friends of Larry's that I had never met before.

Yes. Once I met them at a Christmas party, but I'd never been to their house. They were good people, and simple. He is a chemist and she a housewife. We sat in their backyard by fish pond and watched the fish and turtles eat. We talked, and that is all and yet it seems t here was an anxiety builds up there. Later in bed, I felt the, deep sobs rising inside and choking me. I knew some child was unhappy but I didn't want Larry to know I felt anything but good, and yet he knew. He always knows. He was especially tender in our good night. And I was careful to appreciate him. Long after I thought he was asleep, I lay awake with the great deep sorrow hurting inside, while with my conscious thoughts, I tried to discern where the sorrow was and to speak kind thoughts and words of comfort. Suddenly Larry said "Darling. I live and breathe for you. I wake in the morning and I go to sleep at night with a warm glow because of you. I love you. I do so much hope you can truly know this " The floodgate of tears, opened and I cried in his arms and ,while I cried, I knew that I was happy and oh so wonderfully blessed with him, and yet the child's heart was broken and she cried. Finally, Larry gave me a tranquilizer and I slept, But once I woke and the sadness was still there. This morning I came into the kitchen and as I set out the pans for cooking, I spontaneously burst into tears but checked them. Now he has gone to his work and the girls are dressing for school and I sit at my kitchen table watching the sun rise over the American River a mile away. The trees glisten in the new morning sun and Conda, our young shepherd dog, checks out our yard to see that everything remained the same in the night and life is good, and life is sweet. My little girl is still not quiet and I wonder if I should call Dr. Young and talk for a few minutes. But today is Wednesday and today he does not go to his office so I hesitate to call him. Everything will be okay I am sure.

9 A M
I like the early mornings alone at Garfield when the girls have gone to school and no one is here except myself and the fish and Conda in the yard checking it out to see anything changed overnight and the man who lives in the guesthouse is also gone this morning, and the world is peaceful. Inside things are at rest again. My child has either gone to sleep or is feeling better. In another week, I'll start my fall classes again, but I am very lucky. I'll carry only a half load again and this will leave time for caring for my home, for writing a little, for growing flowers and sewing for Margie and Mike, if I want to."
By Dr. Young.
I received in the mail information about the one under the porch. The author was not identified. The handwriting looked like that of the dreamer. It brought into focus the need to resolve this source of trouble.

"I am far from free. I can't look too clearly for the corners are dark, and things crawl there that I'm not sure of. I tried to stand up straight and walk right but my head bumps the floor. I'm under the porch, you know. There's an underpinnings of lattice worked boards and a little light comes in now and then, but not really enough air gets in.

I've been under this porch for a very long time. I'm hiding here until someone comes for me. Sometimes, I think they never will come. I want to talk, but no one talks to me very often .Not many people have passed this way, and Dr. Young will not get me out.

My eyes are big and brown, and I am skinny. My hair is so straight, not one curl anywhere. My teeth are straight, and good ones and Poppa says I should never have trouble since they are well spaced. But everyone knows I am not pretty. I have a make-believe friend called Nancy who has curls all over her head. I don't know for sure if I'm make believe or not, but I can't get out from under the porch until Bernas comes back for me.

She went away. A long way off to Birmingham in uncle Melvin's car. She screamed and cried, and wanted to stay, but Poppa said 'No'. I now am very angry at Papa. He is very unkind. He lies on the bed at noon time with old Gertie who he brought to live here when mama died. A lot of the trouble is Gertie's fault. She is a hypocrite, and did wrong things. Old Gertie lived over on the hill near Kertain's place. Her husband was a preacher. He had eyes that looked like blue blazes piercing right through you, and his hair was red and blowing around like the flames of fire he roared about. They had three little girls, Bernese, Paulette and Imogene. The first time I knew about them was when Paulette burned to death. She was five years old then and I wasn't four yet. I remember hearing old Gertie screaming that windy November day. I remember seeing Papa run-through the new ground and down through the hollow and up again. A little dot running up Kertain's hill. Mama stood in our yard by the paling fence. She didn't run anywhere. Mama didn't have much run left in her. I guess she had enough of Gertie already and wouldn't have put it past her to cry wolf just so Popa would come running. But when Papa came back later he brought a sad story with him. Old Gertie was doing her washing and like everybody else. She had a fire burning under her black wash pot to boil the water to wash her white socks, sheets and underwear in. She had let Paulette wear a long dress of her sister's maybe because she wanted to and maybe because it was wash day and Paulette didn't have any other clean one. Mama would never let us and get close to the wash pot. Gertie let Paulette and Imogene roast potatoes in the coals of the fire under the pot. Paulette had a stick and was raking around in the fire to tend her potato when the long dress caught on fire. She ran to her mom for help, and the wind was so strong and in the flames rushed up the cheap cotton cloth Gertie tried her dead level best to put out the fire, but Paulette ran screaming down the hill and was burned so badly she died. But she didn't die for 10 days. So when Papa came home and told us, Mama went because it was her duty as a neighbor and also because she had nothing against the preacher and his kids. I went once with Mama to see Paulette. She was a poor little burned looking girl lying naked on a sheet greased with hog lard to keep her from sticking so bad. She whimpered sometimes, but didn't say anything. I tiptoed away from her bed and stood by the door waiting to go home. I knelt by her bed and prayed with the rest before we left. The preacher prayed so loud he was so noisy with God all the time. Later he prayed that way over Mama when she was dying, but it didn't do any good. He didn't talk too plain so he would say, Hank God instead of thank God, but I shouldn't be saying this as that is like making fun of somebody. But I wondered how God felt about being called Hank.

Poor little Paulette lay for a week and had no medicine or dressing. Dr. Middleton went every day to the house and old Gertie and the preacher would meet him at the door and tell him to go away that God would heal Paulette .No man of the devil was coming near her. Finally Graham Hale, who was Justice of the peace and the sheriff went with a warrant and forced them to open the door for Dr. Middleton, but he only shook his head and said he could do nothing. Paulette died that night, and old Gertie and the preacher always said Dr. Middleton killed their baby girl, but I know it wasn't so. So like I said that's about the first thing I remember about old Gertie. Later I found out lots of things about her. I wish Graham Hale and the sheriff would come with a warrant and let me out from under the porch. It's so dark in here, and so lonesome. I can't do anything but remember, and peek outside and long to get out where there is air. I've been under here for times and times again. I guess Dr. Middleton has gone away too. If this house burned down, I would be burned up like Paulette.

Like I said a lot of it is Gertie's fault She was a holy roller and used to get in the spirit and dance up and down the brush arbor ."

When Bernice came for her next appointment, I told her I'd gotten the above letter that I assume had been written automatically as a transcription of thoughts from the child under the porch.

"This child has been under the porch since the father forced Bernas to go to Birmingham. I have previously learned that she dashed there to escape him, and when he drug her out this part dissociated and remained mentally under the porch. She is waiting for someone to come and rescue her. I will do that today if you agree. Do you agree?"

"Yes."

"Close your eyes, and I will ask for her to come out. You may listen in, if you can and want to. Where you are under the porch, you have been waiting for someone to come and get you out. I have come to help you. I think you already know that I am Dr. Young. You have been wanting for me to come for you. I am here with you now. I want to explain something to you so you understand your situation. When your papa found you, as he did, he drug your body out from under the porch but in your mind you did not go. In your mind, you have remained under the porch all this long time. Your body is not under the porch anymore, and your body has kept growing during this time and has grown up now. You will need to get used to being in a grown-up body. Your body is in my office and in a city far away from the home where you were in under the porch. You will need to get used to being in a city not in the home that you were in before your Papa sent you away. Your mind divided into pieces when your papa sent you away and each piece has become like a person of which you are one of them. So, you are one of many persons living in the same body. You will need to get used to that too. This is not going to be easy, but you can do it a little bit at a time. As you have said, you have been under the porch much too long . It is time to come out. The persons are in the body with you and they will help you by explaining the changes and can be your friends. You will learn to live with the changes. Do you want to come out from under the porch now?"

"Yes, it is dark in here, and so lonely."

"Open your eyes now and look at me. I am real and not a dream. You're with me in my office. Look around. You are no longer under the porch. Look at your hands. They are the hands of a woman. Your body has grown into a woman. Look at your body and feel it now. Your body has grown up while you have been under the porch for many years You have a lot to learn and I want to ask one of the people inside to help you learn it. I want you to meet Ruth. Ruth is in the same body with you. Really, She is in the same mind with you. You'll be able to talk with each other, and she can help you understand what is happening. You will have a new home, and there will be children there who can become your friends too. Ruth! Meet the child who has been under the porch. Talk to her and tell her you will teach her to understand her new home. Tell her you will be with her and take care of her.(Pause) Now I will return the consciousness to Bernice.

Bernice! Wake up now. I have had the child come out from under the porch and asked Ruth to help her learn her new home. She has a lot to get used to. She will be confused and anxious until she gets adjusted. I know this is going to be troubling but eventually she will be much better off than trapped under the porch. I hope all of you will be patient and supportive of her. I hope your mind has been listening to what has happened and will help you understand what has been done."

The last contact I had from Bernice was letter in which she said she had retired because of heart trouble and had returned to the place of her childhood and was hoping to rebuild her childhood home. I wrote back saying I was glad to hear from but very sorry she had heart trouble. I did not hear back for months so, I wrote a letter to her last address. It was returned to me. I have tried numerous ways to contact her and have failed. The postmaster did not have any information about her. A letter to the last address I had from California was returned to me. I fear she died from a heart attack.

Bernice's Poetry

You have the most beautiful eyes,
The most handsome face,
The loveliest voice, and stride and pace.
The wonderful wisdom your mind relates.
As you listen to people and guide their fates.
Your hands are strong, with a grip sincere
and I fancy now that I can hear,
you say to me while in despair,
There's a lot of good tied up in there,
Let's talk and remember and evaluate,
The things of the past and let's re-create
The scenes that you buried in self-defense,
And see how you've suffered the consequence,
And then from the rubbish, debris of the past,
We'll make a new life and cement it fast,
With a good foundation and sturdy walls
And it'll be a strong building,
one that won't fall.
I love you doctor,
I'm not ashamed to say,
For it's not in a selfish or sensual way,
But I love you as a child its father adores,
Or as I love God,
and I know the scores of patients
who look to you feel the same.

And we lower our voice
when we say your name.
For we feel a reverence, a love, devotion,
To you, whose voice is a healing lotion.
B.W.

The earth is parched dry,
Great schisms appear on the surface
With all the balm engulfed within,
There's no dampness to give the grasses drink,
No harrowed soil where roots can sink.
All the earth is parched and dry,
Life struggles feebly under the blazing sky.
Where are the clouds
To shield the earth from desert sun?
When will the coolness come
The heat of the day be past and gone?
Is God still watching from above?
A god of vengeance of or love?
The one who breathed the breath of life,
Said, "Wretched one, now you know your strife."
Unwind yourself, relax with ease.
There is no way for <u>all</u> to please.
So be whatever thing you are,
But be that thing with ease and grace,
And let the tension all unwind
And wrinkles leave your face.
Raise up your head and be collected,
There is no need, someone has said,
For you to feel neglected.
.

Nighttime, all is soft, serene.
Nighttime, I hear the lovely call again,
Nighttime, when quietness cushions all,
Nighttime, I think sometimes I hear you call.

Hold me in your mind at least
While our necessary parting reigns,
Try to feel my presence in early morning

In evening's hush again.
I'll love you forever it is true
Through many years and miles.

A voice so clear, so sweet, so true,
Vibrating waves that seem to come from you,
Oh to hold you just for one more time
And feel you lips so tender pressed to mine.

Searching for just a tiny trace
Of love or affection in your face,
I turn with a knowledge
Like stabs of pain,
And I feel the gathering Of a salty rain.

Tell me all about yourself,
Your hopes, your dreams
Your childhood life,
I feel a need to turn from me,
Forget myself awhile, be free.
Free from the effort, free from trying
From morbid talk of death and dying.
Let me be your support awhile
I the mother, you the child.
Too long I've had a passive role,
Let me now be well and bold.
For I am one with strength to live
With wisdom, kindness, love to give,
Perhaps someday again I'll climb,
But give me here a little time.

THE PRISON THEATER

Curtain, filmy, misty, thick with dust,
Cobwebs cover the open places,
The stage is veiled, and all shut out,
All but the fading faces.
The play was cast decades ago,
Ancient, old and out of date,
Lines forgotten, learned again.
Always wait.
The players scolding, bitter, sour,
Impatient for the opening hour.
Sometimes they peep beyond the curtain,
Past empty chairs and open door.
Into the busy town, and listen for the sound,
Of footsteps coming near, and all they hear
Is people going past,
Laughter in the distance, fading out at last.
They try the lock, the door is tight,
Windows closed, not even light
Can penetrate the dirty pane,
They wait in vain.
Time hasn't seemed to move ahead,
They need no water, wine or bread,
A restless feeling hints that it is growing late,
Enthusiasm blocked like stagnant water turns to hate,

I built a structured world
Where I could go,
When all outside was in chaos,
And I could know contentment.
A release from life awhile,
I could retire and be a child.
I stayed too long one day
Within my safe retreat,
The raindrops beat in vain
Upon a painted window pane.
My world was oh so safe from outer strife
Within this structured world,
I lost my life.

I wouldn't say anything is out of reach
Farther away than you own arm's length,
Or heavier than you can carry
When lifted by your strength.

It's not enough that one can strive
To aid or still another soul
Map out his path or choose his fold.
For surely as there is a sky
Each soul is given wings to fly.

The right to live?
You ask a question such as that?
What does it mean?
It is so that you may glean
A bit of wisdom
From the ages
And merge yourself
With long gone sages.
It is a trust,
This right to live
To love your fellow man
And so to give.
You say you've nothing
For a gift,
Between mankind and you
There is a right?
But that's what life is for
To bridge the break
Until with others
You can give and take.

Happiness, that elusive thing that all seek
The poor and rich, the strong and weak
Is always walking just ahead upon a hill
But all can reach it if they will.

Is love this thing we're always reaching for

With wishful thinking, strong desire
But who can love with passions strong
In isolation all day long?

As flowers grow, as rivers flow
Out from your heart and let them go
The little fears and binding cord
That holds them there in one great hoard.

But who would want a thing like me?
What could I offer were I free?
A peaceful heart, a purpose bold
Support for yet another soul.

One thing I will no longer be is <u>good</u>.
Convention can bind or bend or break
A fragile vine
But not my <u>stake</u>!
I claim the right to be whatever on this earth I can
<u>Equal</u> unto every man.
So take your verbs, your metaphors, your nouns
And I will take the form I've found.
To please myself
And if you choose to walk with me
Lay down your load and then be free!

Where is my faith?
Where is the faith I once held tight
Regardless of storm or darkened night?
Gone as the wind in frantic haste
Leaving my soul a wretched waste.

Reach once more for a place to hold
Look you deeper into your soul
Find a place within your breast
Where your hopes and dreams still rest.
Where the cares of daytime living
Melt in tranquil love forgiving.
Where your spirit finds its shield

Where your cup can be refilled.

Happiness, that elusive thing that all seek
The poor and rich, the strong and weak
Is always walking just ahead upon a hill
But all can reach it if they will.

Is love this thing we're always reaching for
With wishful thinking, strong desire
But who can love with passions strong
In isolation all day long?

As flowers grow, as rivers flow
Out from your heart and let them go
The little fears and binding cord
That holds them there in one great hoard.

But who would want a thing like me?
What could I offer were I free?
A peaceful heart, a purpose bold
Support for yet another soul.

The sun is shinning brightly
No clouds deface the sky
Only one, a lovely one
Is slowly passing by
Downy clouds of whiteness
Like the little rising fawn
Who ascended to the heavens
With the breaking of the dawn
The storm has passed
And left the earth washed clean

There was no storm,
Was just a passing dream you had
Your only thought the lightening flashed
And thought the wind was rushing past,
You thought the rain fell from above,
You thought the trees bent down in pain

And that you called for help in vain,
You only thought, my soul, you died
That God ignored you when you cried.
Was just a dream you had that has past
And now you're safely home at last.
And that the thunder scared the dove,

The beauty of a single rose
The love of God that people know
The laughter of a tiny face
The living proof of Godly grace.

There are some things we need to say
To one we love so much this day
But miles and hours are in between
Some things we'll never say, we mean.
. . . . .
What is the greatest thing on earth
To live alone or to give birth?
Oh God. Let creativity be.
Let it move and pass through me.
To love as much as life is long
And always sing a happy song

MY CHILD
Child of my heart
When I look at you
I perceive the depths of this ocean blue
For secrets lie within you deep
Secrets of life for you to keep.

Thoughts and plans for future goals
Hope for a thousand other souls
A restless spirit, a stirring need
To look for other lambs to feed.

Child, you will grow and flourish too
For the world's in need of one like you,
A need for love to give, receive
For you are now tomorrow's eve.

God, it's been such a long time
Since I prayed.
I've been around I'm sure, but
I can't say where
Somehow I have a feeling you were there.
Watching, helping, waiting
Until I got all untangled
From the web of confusion.
Now that's in the past,
And I'm ready to go to work again,
I think I'm wiser now.

I don't want to underrate myself,
I can do some good I'm sure,
Somewhere.
I need to learn to assert myself more and speak up.
Silence is golden but it also signifies dullness, at times.

As I make a second try at life
And find the thing I missed at first, I'm glad.
My heart could almost burst with joy.
I walked alone, the night was dark

My path confused as in a maze,
I pushed from one entangled growth
Into another daze.
The winds lashed fierce
The storm clouds grew,
My faith was pierced and almost failed
But always yet a glimmer
Of a distant light prevailed.
Throughout the long nocturnal flight
Searching for freedom in the night,
I battled, weakened, fought and cried,
And fearing most my faith had died.
When at last in resignation
I tried again for concentration,
My ailing spirit, humbled there
Was lifted by another's prayer.
I knew the barricade was gone
That kept me from my Father's throne,
And once again the night was day,
I wasn't lost . . . for I could pray.
Restored at least after an exile
Into the night, brought again
By the power of the priesthood
Into God's merciful light.

December 2nd
I have so much conceit
Conceit I am – inside, outside
Wrong side, right side
Good and strong and
Honest conceit!

Conceit enough to spread
In many directions

Sprinkle it generously on
The weak part of me – on
The little dolls that were
Only part people – that could see – only weakly.

Part people they were – and
They were me. Part people –
Life is too hard for part people.
They need to merge and be –
Strong like me –

(note December 10ᵗʰ)

This conceit I think at the time
Written might have been
"self-esteem" – I felt <u>good</u>.

December 2ⁿᵈ

Come into my forest –
I'll show you my trees –
If you listen carefully
You'll feel the breeze –
And hear the motion?

Gods we are in my forest –

Bare is my soul –
Aged, forever aged –
Never growing old –

Standing alone in my forest
Apart and forlorn –
Is a tree I used forever
Until it was ragged and torn –

The back is hanging useless,
The limbs are brittle and tired –
My tree, my tree, my used one
I'll love you a special way,
I'll give you a generous
Handful of blossoms every day
And showers in spring and summer

To keep the dust away
In cooler seasons my loved one,
I'll give you a mossy
Coat, and stars above one.

January 1960
I'm in no mood
for discouragement
I feel fine
If facts are black
Then close the door
Leave me with thoughts divine.
Leave me alone to walk the stairs
Of my imagination
To see the sky and feel the wind
Enjoy God's creation.
. . . . .
But I am tired; My aching back and
Arms and feet
Tell you to quiet down
You've met defeat.
I say you cannot dull my spirit
Or make me settle down
One day I'll leave this dusty building
And walk in town
Where people are
And all is gay.

Invitation To Retreat
A chill and restless wind,
both calm and wild
Rings out and calls
to you lost child;
It's voice is whispers
like the grass
Hearken now
and hear it pass,
And hear it call
and hear it sigh
Now call aloud
and answer back
Listen now .
. your faith is slack.
Come to the woods

where grow the flowers
And where the ground
is wet from showers
Where trees
in majesty protect
The small things
that all else reject.
Come to the woods
and play lost child
Come to the woods
and rest awhile.

Long grows the night,
and huddled white
Against a clump of brush.
A child sleeps.
There sings a thrush
In early morning
for the child, who
Came into the woods
to rest awhile.
There is no other way
to look for peace
Retreat from life,
find your release.
Long is the day
and happy in
the wooded glen
Remember us lost child
come back again.
Huddled in your rigid fear
you sit
You know the way
to come, and yet
You hold those things
that to your heart are dear,
But come to us,
our fortune share.
Come lost child.

Learn with us to sing
For winter's past
and it is Spring.
Violets bloom and
dogwood flowers in the wood
Come back to us lost child
oh that you would.
You have no need for
those who hold
Material things
and seek for gold
Come from the woods,
lost child, lost soul.
Take shelter and this rock
will keep you warm
Your clothes are gone,
your feet are bare.
Your flesh is bleeding,
burs mat your ragged hair.
You have a place with us,
look this way once again
And when you come,
come with the wind
Come with this wind,
and sing with us
the song of spirits
In the wooded life.
Abide with us lost child,
avoid the strife

Lost Love
Searching for just a tiny trace
Of love or affection in your face
I turned with a knowledge
Like stabs of pain
And I felt the gathering
Of a salty rain.

. . . . .

February 1961

A house divided cannot stand
Here or in another land
Cohesion must be the rule of thumb
Small additions make a larger sum.

Reconciliation

We sing a song, a song we sing today
For fathered now in tolerance we stay
No rule is harsh, no burden great
Together we will share a common fate.

Dreams

Throughout the night dreams came
Like movies on a screen before my eyes
Scenes pass, and always there somewhere
Upon the screen . . . you are.
I see your hands so near you are,
Yet you are out of reach so far.
Sometimes you bend your face to mine,
I almost brushed your lips a dozen times,
I reach to touch your face, you're gone
And with you goes the dream, the song.

Long after the evening shadows fall
And when the last small piercing call
Echoes across the desert plain
We feel a pain.

Not a pain of hurt, so much as sorrow
Because we know there's no tomorrow
To spend with you in love sincere,

Your love is dead, so all is drear.
We know no more your touch we'll feel,
And yet . . . we know the hurt will heal,
As things will do when time has passed,
For nothing in this life will last.

Wading on, far past the safety zone
Into the sea.
Trust I keep, even in waters
Marked deep.
In a current swift, plunging deeper,
Deeper in,
Until the body stretches bends.
The sea is vast, so very great
I want to hold his hand
But that can wait.
I will not pull him in with me
He has a world, this is my sea.
For if we hold on longer tight
There'd come a darkness like the night
And wind and waves would dash in turn
And to my sorrow I would lean
That love had perished in the flight
Of cold and stormy rain filled night.
The sea is mine, I must go on
For I have passed the safety zone.
. . . . .
The cutting of the strings that bind
A soul unto another soul, is pain.
More hurt than any eye can see
But I'm impatient to be free!

Easter 1960
April 17

Reminded once again that there is life,
Life unlimited – of course we live on
after this short earth span passes away.
We all join in with God and his one long eternal day.
Our trivial fears and ills and short retreat
into the past are just a link
That joins our life
and holds it fast to God.

Joy and peace and faith and basic good
in man will triumph yet.
For God does live and lives inside
the heart of man, emerging when he can.
We ever strive to break the tomb
and roll away the stone to let a flow of life
Come forth that life can ere go on.

I almost felt your face near mine
Your breathing prickled up my spine
But when I turned response to show,
You weren't there.

Your arms encircled me, I felt
That without caution I would melt
My arms reached up to hold you now,
Your weren't there.

Dreams, fantasy of a lonely soul
Who wants fulfillment of a goal
A secure place, someone to love
Patience, hope.

Hold me my beloved one
And let me feel the strength of your embrace
Let me be near you,
And touch your hair and stroke your face,
And at your arm be tight and steady.

I want to be near you, for I am ready
To give myself to you.

Oh let me sit beside you my beloved one.
I am so proud that you have chosen me.
I want the world to know that we are one,
That I belong to you.
The noblest one beneath God's sun.
Oh friend and lover ever true.
My heart beats just for you.

Nighttime, all is soft, serene.
Nighttime, hear the lonely call again.
Nighttime, when quietness cushions all.
Nighttime, I hear you call.

Voice so clear, so sweet, so true.
On vibrating air they come from you.
Oh now to hold you one more time
And feel your lips so tender press to mine.

I think of you when the harsh winds call
When clouds are dark and rain drops fall
Then the coldest storm of a winter's night
Is calmed like a balmy summer's light.

When all is dark and I fear to tread
Where the unknown leads and I feel a dread
I think of you and my courage lifts.

. . . . .

June 25, 1961
I cry just one small drop, one tear,
As softly on the stairs of time I hear
Your footsteps in the distance growing faint.
Go from my life completely if you go,
Don't haunt my memories in the night or day.
But as you pass and travel on another way,

Help me to cut the strings before you go on
Through the years of life and time
I'll suffer so.

When midnight came and all the earth was dark
as far as eye could see,
I felt the one in bondage stirring,
impatient to be free.
Scrub timber and underbrush,
and under that the boulders.
Above, the fury of the storm
seemed resting on my shoulders.
The angry clouds with all the rain
shut out the stars and moon.
Yet still above the raging of the storm,
the bound one whispered, "soon."
The tree was tall and strong,
but trembled with the rest,
And begged the storm have mercy,
small birds were in the nest
Motionless, quiet, they cling
and dare not make a sound.
Though brave, they fear the raging storm
will dash them to the ground
Intense and heavy,
turmoil, strife and flight
Deeper, sinking lower,
almost gone into the night.
And then the clouds break open
and darkness turns to light.
The angry wind has passed away
, a breeze is lightly teasing
And with the passing of the storm ,
life once again is pleasing.
Climb high upon the hilltop
where trouble cannot rise
And watch the birds take to their wings
and soar into the skies,
It's good to know that

when the midnight comes
and all seems vain,
In just one minute morning
comes and it is light again.

"Your face is strangely familiar," I said,
bending over the cadaver,
inspecting the dead.
I've seen you somewhere along the way
On the sandy beach,
in the ocean's spray,
In the wind as it rustled
through the tall pine trees
In the mountain stream and the mystic sea,
We walked in a long forgotten day
Thru an open meadow in the grasses sway,
We found a world where none could be
Excluding them all, just you and me
It was long ago, and the time has past,
Since we were friends and friends so fast.
And now we meet in this lonely place,
And I look down into your sleeping face,
I wonder where we chanced to part,
As sadness wells within my heart
For the past is gone, beyond recall,
When we built an empire
that was doomed to fall, and
Now I walk alone.

Hold me my beloved one
And let me feel the strength of your embrace
Let me be near you,
And touch your hair and stroke your face,
And at your arm be tight and steady.
I want to be near you, for I am ready
To give myself to you.

Oh let me sit beside you my beloved one.
I am so proud that you have chosen me.

I want the world to know that we are one,
That I belong to you.
The noblest one beneath God's sun.
Oh friend and lover ever true.
My heart beats just for you.

Nighttime, all is soft, serene.
Nighttime, hear the lonely call again.
Nighttime, when quietness cushions all.
Nighttime, I hear you call.

Voice so clear, so sweet, so true.
On vibrating air they come from you.
Oh now to hold you one more time
And feel your lips so tender press to mine.

Heroes die on the battlefield
While cowards live.
Why is it always just the best
That's asked to give?
That's asked to sacrifice and fall
In death so vain?
While those are left
Who will not strive to walk
The flagstones we have lain.

If love's the song of life
Then sing it loud
And sing it clear.
Don't let it be
All dampened with a tear.

. . . . .

You're the damndest fool
That life has made
You want to love
But you're afraid

.So full of wisdom
Yet none is wise at all.
We try, but still we fall.
At best we only try to understand
Ourselves and then our fellow man.
How small we are,
how great sometimes we feel
And center all the world
around our own being.
While value judgments fly
like bits of nature toward the sky

The cutting of the strings that bind
A soul unto another soul
So painful. More pain by far than eyes can see
But I'm impatient to be free.
I bleed a little it's true
Each time I snip another string
But I must, I must
And still not lose my trust.

God, you heard my cry for help
And sent to me your greatest one
And now again I cry for aid
To help me leave him unafraid.

May 26, 1961

Dawning of light comes to mankind
It's getting nearer daylight
Such a long, dark walk through years of night
But it was a half pleasant walk.

Love makes free the soul
Unbinds the string
And warms the cold.
Love long you eluded me
I held you back
Until one turned the key

Then all restraint
All fear is gone
And you are free

Releasing me from bondage tight
Oh love, I see
I see the light
I see the dawning of a day, a day of joy
Not far away
I will go forth
In good trust and unafraid
To win the battle of the day.

I wish, my friend,
that you wouldn't try
to make me be something else.
I like me.
I think it's nice to just be kind.
Isn't that enough?
Must we worry about other "stuff"
Like good grades or impressing others
Or building egos?
I'm just like a stream that flows
In a quiet manner
Life isn't a game we compete in,
Or I'm not competing.
Just living, sleeping, eating.
What's better to be had than
A warm house,
When all the children are asleep,
Quiet – like a mouse.
And you know they're safe through one more day,
With their books and toys put away.
And you get a book and settle down
Now what's better?

One thing I will no
Longer be is good.
I will be free.

Convention can bind,
Or bend or break
A fragile vine
But not my stake
I claim the right to
Be whatever on this earth I want to be
I am equal to any man.

February 14, 1961
One does with life
What one must do
And I must share
My thought with you.

Throughout the days,
The moments fleet repast
And leaves a shadow
Or a print that lasts.

Give me a place
On earth to be of use
And I will serve with
Joy and not abuse.

Where among these ruins that time has left
Can I find my life, my own true self?
Where's the child that used to play
In the meadows grassy way?
Where's the one who failed to grow?
Where's the one no one could know?
How can I, who feel such need for these the lost,
Bring them back to life at any cost?
Be not weary any longer, I will help you to grow stronger.
Though I do not understand why you linger underground.
I can open wide the way for you to come home to stay.
We are one, we stand in mutual need.
For each other to live and be freed.

Perhaps the most one can hope for are the little joys that fill our

Days. A mark of wisdom here or there,
A friendly chat, a kiss, a book.

Out of the dark my child you came
Hungry and cold without a name
Alone, so still so small, in need.
I turned you out one time – in greed.
But now I reach my hand for you.
Come to me now and let me do the
Things my heart has said before.
Come on my child.

Write, observe, poet laureate
Seclusive
Not interested in socializing but
Likes to relate through writing
People and things interesting to observe
Sensitive to criticism,
feelings easily hurt, withdrawn

I was waiting for you
In the springtime,
Down at the foot of the hill,
And the forest was dark around me,
And the wildness brought a chill.

Nowhere on earth was such beauty
Such splendor of tender hue,
And the birds sang some songs
As they made their nests
While I waited for you.

You told me to wait in the canyon,
Where the cool spring water seeps
From the mossy ground.
So I descended the hillside to get there,
And you had forgotten, I found.

I waited there in the shadows

Til the day had turned to night,
Til the world around was darkened
Excepting the pale moonlight.

Sometimes I feel closer
to you when we're apart.
It's then that I feel free
to listen, listen to my heart.

From night, September 23, 1964

Midnight shadows fall from a half hidden moon
Clouds but never rain – just pain.
Never can this prison wall be broken down
Unless a key is found.
I cry inside the prison wall
I am not free. I cannot be.
Outside I see a world go by
A little bird, a blue of sky
But none so loathful, none but I.
Fat, layers of fat,
and these make that
Thick prison wall.
I am near dead,
please hear me call.

I thought I loved a robin
With beauty i
on its breast
With gentle eye
and tender beak
that gave me rest

I was happy in my private room
With dreams of peaceful flow
But when I looked again I found
My robin was a crow.

January 1962
God, I need to find the strength within,
That I must somewhere, still possess,
Give me now the sight to find it,
That I might be quiet and rest.

Cries my soul in starving hunger
For another soul to need,
Now Dear God, I humbly ask you
Please help me your voice to heed.

It's love, this thing we're always reaching for
With wistful thinking, strong desire,
But who can love with passions strong
In isolation all day long?
As flowers grow, and rivers flow
Cut now the strings and let them go.
The little fears and binding cord
That holds your trust is one big hoard.
But who would want a thing like me?
What could I offer were I free?

A trusting heart, a purpose bold
Support for yet another soul.

I'm as lost tonight as ever lost has been,
I think sometimes I'm found at last and then
Aside from all the gain I think I've made
I find that deep inside, I'm still afraid.

But not afraid forever; just awhile
You feel the shadows of the jungle wild.
Tomorrow you will smile again and see
That hope will win the fear and you'll be free.

Complaining of time that's spent
to make a life like new
Is like the weeping,
for a morning dew.

For as the dew
refreshes earth that's dry
The time will strengthen
up your wings to fly.

Look backwards only
for a tiny look
At where you've been,
and where you'll never be again,
Time moves on
and so will you,
Open the door
and go on through.

Reaching back for memories
Looking at the past
For precious gems guarded
Within the heart so fast.
Good times around the hearth fire
The back log snaps and crack
Papa rocks in the corner chair
The one with the creaking back.

Outside the winter snow falls softly
Silently covering the cold bare ground
White, soft and beautifully quiet,
A shy bell the only sound.

Ice freezes on the screened back porch
The dogs huddle close in the shed
The coziest place for a child to be
Is warm – in a snug safe bed.

Good night my child said mother
And gently tucked in
The downy bright
blue patchwork quilt
Under the little chin.

She closed the door so softly
After putting out the light
Secure in a mother's knowledge
That the child was safe for the night.

It was like a dream passed over
Or the breath of an angel near.
It was silent; oh so silent
No sound that could reach the ear.

Sorrow hangs over
the valley like a fog.
Clouds pregnant with rain
wished to give up the burden
That they hold.
And unprotected
and alone in the valley
Is my soul.

Long winding path – path of life
There's nothing more to fear;
For with the help of ones concerned
The dreaded now is dear.

Sad the fact that steps must part,
Because of one whose reasons fail
Because in strict unbending ways
He still demands – prevails.

Insists that yet a battle rages
Inside a life where love has found
A place at last to dwell and grow
Where all is calm
and rivers flow in peace.
And sadder still that in his way
This man is good and kind and strong,
So soon forget that he has passed
This transit in years that only
Late have gone.

How can the human spirit grow and
Progress as God meant that it should do
Unless there be a meeting of the old and new?
And one descends as snow drops do.

I ask of him – where is the boy,
The one that struggled for his faith
Sought and ardently defended
by his childhood father.

The day is new

You are so good
So kind
How can I find
The words to say.

The words that are
In my heart today?
I would reach out
And hold your hand
I understand.

My love
I give my heart
My life to thee.

The Song of Life

Love, more than any thing
Leave to the tired the weary bring
Hope and all that makes life good

06/15/1961

tell me all about yourself
your hopes, your dreams
your childhood life.
I feel a need to turn from mine
Forget myself awhile, be free.
From effort and from trying
From morbid talk of death and crying.
Let me be your support awhile
I the mother – you the child.
I've had too long the passive role
Now let me be both will and bold.
Treat me as one with strength to live
With wisdom, kindness, love to give
Don't urge me climb
Just give me time.

You just might try
But try in vain you'll find
To drive such memories
From your mind.
Sweet, painful, tender bliss
Awakened by your first real kiss.
Arms lean, strong and tight
Whispered sweetness, all is right
So right.

He says, "I'm a bridge you walk upon"
To reach more solid ground
And I think I'm very lucky
Such a friend that I have found.

But alas, he is a toll bridge
There's no coin inside my purse
So I chant the old worn phrase
"Money is just one big curse."

It was said, "forget the price,

pay on the other side"
but I then can curse myself
and my stubborn willful pride.

So I wrestle with my conscience
Should I then a drifter be,
Or a fool who kept her pride
Drowned with honor in the sea?

There's a deep and hidden sorrow
In the eyes that never cries
In the heart so heavy
Like storm filled winter skies.
A yearning and an aching
For a need so long unfilled
A dammed up source
of something
That would yield
From a charge of murder
When appealed.

Editorial comment:
The loss of her mother,
her father and and
her childhood home
appear to be expressed
in expressions of loss
and longing.The poems
of being loved may
have been written
after Larry came
into her life.The
time the poems were
written is not reflected
in the order of their
appearance above.

RECOMMENDED READING

The Structure of Magic, volumes 1 and 2.
Richard Bandler and John Grinder.

Clinical Perspectives on Multiple Personality Disorder.
Richard Kluft

The Satir Model.
Virginia Satir et al

The Wisdom of Milton Erickson.
Richard Havens.

The Answer Within.
Lankton and lankton

Recreating Your Self.
Nancy Napier

Sybil
Flora Schreiber

Magic in Practice
Garner Thomson

The Memory Book
Harry Lorayne

www.ingramcontent.com/pod-product-compliance
Lightning Source LLC
Chambersburg PA
CBHW061304280526
45784CB00002B/893